SHAOLIN LONG FIST KUNG FU

少林長拳

SHAOLIN LONG FIST KUNG FU

by YANG JWING-MING
and JEFFERY A. BOLT

DISCLAIMER

Please note that the publisher of this instructional book is NOT RESPONSIBLE in any manner whatsoever for any injury which may occur by reading and/or following the instructions herein.

It is essential that before following any of the activities, physical or otherwise, herein described, the reader or readers should first consult his or her physician for advice on whether or not the reader or readers should embark on the physical activity described herein. Since the physical activities described herein may be too sophisticated in nature, it is *essential that a physician be consulted.*

©UNIQUE PUBLICATIONS INC., 1982
All rights reserved
Printed in the United States of America
ISBN: 0-86568-020-5
Library of Congress No.: 80-54832

UP UNIQUE
PUBLICATIONS
4201 VANOWEN PLACE, BURBANK, CA 91505

8 9 0 D 85

ACKNOWLEDGEMENTS

The writers wish to thank Yang's classmate Master Nelson Tsou and his students for sharing and supplying their vast wealth of documents on Wu Su which they have collected over the years. The authors also wish to thank Vidas Gvozdzius, Cosmin Theodore, and Rod Engle who helped with the book.

To Master Li Mao-Ching

PREFACE

Chinese Kung Fu has long been a mystery to the Western world. Only recently has it come into the light along with other martial systems from the East. Although Kung Fu has received more attention, it still suffers in one important respect: too many Westerners confuse Chinese Kung Fu with other Eastern martial systems. In the West all Chinese, Japanese, and Korean styles are amalgamated into the general terms "Kung Fu" or "Karate." An emphasis on pointing out the distinctions between the systems is very important because each system or style has its own approach to martial arts. Although some aspects of Kung Fu may be similar to other styles such as Karate or Tae Kwan Do, Kung Fu remains unique in its theory and application.

Although no definitive definition of Kung Fu can be formed due to the diversity and vastness of the art, the best possible definition, for now, is that Kung Fu is a specific martial system developed over three thousand years of Chinese history. This point cannot be overemphasized. Kung Fu is the flower of Chinese culture; one cannot hope to understand Kung Fu without also coming to understand the Chinese view of themselves and the world. China is one of the few countries where culture and martial arts have mixed and influenced each other to a significant extent.

Because a vast culture has produced an equally vast martial system, no single book can hope to explain anything except points of a rudimentary nature. Therefore, this book will introduce and focus on the elementary and middle levels of Shao Lin Long Fist. The authors hope later to publish advanced volumes on the barehand techniques and weapons of Long Fist. But even with the material in this volume, a martial artist will have to practice at least five years before he can master them. Hopefully, later volumes can present more in-depth material for experienced martial artists. Before going into the contents of this book, it will be useful to understand the motivations behind the writing of this volume on Long Fist.

The first reason for publishing this book is to show and explain the true traditional aspects of Chinese Kung Fu. Too many students enter a martial arts studio which advertises itself as "Kung Fu" and end up learning some style which is not Chinese Kung Fu. Besides misadvertising themselves, these studios leave the student with the impression that he has actually learned Kung Fu, when in fact, he has not. Hopefully, this book can help correct such practices.

In America, because relatively few people study, teach, and practice Chinese Kung Fu, a book emphasizing one style can help bring out more in-depth information. As a result, the authors believe that because of the scarcity of traditional Wu Su stylists, a need exists for a broad-based organization which will be a focus or center for research, practice, discussion, dissemination of information, and other activities relating to traditional Chinese Kung Fu. In particular, the authors hope that the organization will lead the way in establishing a comprehensive martial library which will contain books, pamphlets, movies, etc., on every division of Kung Fu. In addition, the authors hope that this organization will spread Kung Fu through demonstrations, newsletters, and public exposure of famous martial artists and their achievements.

The last reason for publishing, and maybe the most important, is the question of the survival of Kung Fu. Currently, the pressure and the hustle and bustle of modern living leaves little time for the study and development of Kung Fu ideas and skills; and time is the one vital element needed to grow and develop martial skills. In ancient times it was believed that a person had to practice at least ten years before mastery of a certain style was achieved. Few people are willing to practice for ten years while also coping with the problems of career and family. For this reason the authors hope to show modern society that Kung Fu deserves to be classified as an important form of art, and its preservation is of extreme importance.

In terms of showing and preserving knowledge for the students and instructors of Long Fist, this volume can provide an invaluable aid for teaching sequences and explaining other aspects of the style. A new student under the proper instruction can use this book and future volumes as aids in assimilating Long Fist much more accurately and quickly. The student who has studied a Chinese Kung Fu style similar to Long Fist for at least five years may, under a good master, use this volume to reach the middle level of Long Fist within a short period—provided he diligently practices. For practitioners of other non-Kung Fu styles such as Karate, Hapkido, or Tae Kwan Do, to gain elementary and middle level proficiency may take much longer because students familiar with styles other than those in Kung Fu must start from the basics.

This book lays a foundation for the advanced stages of Long Fist in terms of giving the student of Kung Fu a grounding in fundamental and intermediate knowledge and skills. The first chapter will introduce the history of Kung Fu, martial morality, and a section on the "common knowledge" shared by Chinese martial artists. Martial morality is an especially important section dealing with the essence of Kung Fu: the heart and mind of the martial artist.

The second chapter will introduce fundamental starting points such as warming up, stretching, stances, hand forms, punches, kicks, power and speed training, and striking zones. A unique feature of this chapter will be the section on power and speed training. In that section, methods for developing speed and power are taken from different divisions and explained in detail. Because Kung Fu is defensive fighting, a number of essential techniques for dodging and escaping will be explained along with the theories of "distance."

The third chapter will introduce the fundamental "sequences" (Tan) of Long Fist*. Along with the description of each sequence, the use or "solutions" (*Gieh*) of each technique will be shown. Very rarely have books on Chinese Wu Su shown the particular uses of the techniques within a sequence. In fact, many traditional instructors will not teach the solutions until the student has been practicing for two to three years. By explaining many things which have been long considered secret, it is hoped that the potential student will learn faster because he can see the theory behind the methods. By making it clear that each technique has a specific use, the sequence is shown to be an evolved series of beautiful, yet useful, self-defense techniques.

---

* Some people use the words "set" or "forms" for Tan. In this book the authors prefer to use the word "sequence" because it describes the basic movement of a Tan more accurately.

The fourth chapter will build upon the third by presenting two middle level Long Fist sequences. The techniques at this level are more complex. Although other middle level sequences exist, the ones presented in the fourth chapter are representative of the basic skills needed to master this stage of Long Fist. In particular, since Long Fist has been affected by many Northern divisions (see Chapter 1 for the history of Long Fist), the sequence called Shaw Fu Ien will teach and display elements from Northern Praying Mantis.

Finally, the fifth chapter will show some of the fighting theory and techniques of Long Fist. This chapter will explain more fully the practical implications of the concepts *distance* and *open door*. In addition, a few training procedures called *fighting forms* will be explained. The fighting forms are training exercises that constantly repeat one or more techniques continuously. Besides basic training procedures for free fighting, this chapter will also discuss strategies against different styles of fighters.

With the basic foundation presented in this book, the martial artist and the martial scholar can use this volume for research or for practical study. After reaching a certain level, the advanced martial artist can begin to investigate and create new forms and ideas. Many people mistakenly assume that innovation is not a part of traditional Kung Fu. This is far from the truth. What is true is that innovation can take place only in a context of a system that is first learned and mastered. The authors hope that the information presented in this book can help in the progress of Kung Fu.

TABLE OF CONTENTS

CHAPTER 1
GENERAL
INTRODUCTION

INTRODUCTION AND SHAO LIN HISTORY

A good place to start in the study of Kung Fu is to understand the meaning of the word itself. Kung Fu literally means energy (*Kung*) and time (*Fu*). Many Westerners have mistakenly thought that Kung Fu, as such, meant some sort of fighting system. In actuality, any skill, talent, or technique that requires patience (energy and time) is called Kung Fu; in this way a violinist who constantly practices and thus achieves a high level of competence may be said to have "Kung Fu." In terms of common usage the everyday Chinese word for martial arts is *Wu Su* which means *martial technique*.

In China, the word Kung Fu came to be identified with the martial arts because according to Chinese tradition, proficiency in a martial system required at least ten years of devoted practice; the Chinese martial artist thus needed an extreme amount of Kung Fu. The martial artist who constantly practiced became the symbol for the dedication, energy and patience required to live up to the ideals of Kung Fu. In time, Wu Su came to be known as Wu Kung, which means "martial Kung Fu" or more simply "Kung Fu."

As another approach to the understanding of Kung Fu, we now turn to a point mentioned in the preface which stated that Kung Fu is a distinctive outgrowth of Chinese culture. No other society of people has supported and endorsed a system of martial arts as have the Chinese. Historically, Kung Fu in China was an integral part in the education of scholars and the leaders of government. The Chinese people placed great value on the practice of Kung Fu because they felt it to be the great teacher of respect, patience, humility, and morals as a whole: all those qualities which a scholar and leader must live by. Kung Fu was thus cultivated in the highest circles of scholarship and government. In many paintings the great philosopher Confucius can be seen with a sword at his side; the sword symbolized that he possessed moral habits of mind and body through the study of martial arts. From the poorest peasant to the greatest emperor, the possession of Kung Fu skills was believed to be the mark of a good individual. In essence, Chinese culture and Chinese Kung Fu cannot be separated without doing irreparable damage to either one.

With the intimate involvement of Kung Fu in Chinese culture, one fact becomes extremely important. Kung Fu, like Chinese culture, is over three thousand years old. During those three thousand years every possible aspect of martial theory and technique has been exposed, developed, and practiced. This long history of practical development has made Kung Fu one of the most complete systems of martial arts in existence. The long history of Kung Fu is a great asset since those thousands of years have seen a continual growth in theory and technique. To reject three thousand years of experience is to reject everything of proven value.

Turning now to the history of Wu Su, we find that there have been many styles, but the greatest in terms of organization, over-all training methods, and morality was developed out of a Buddhist monastery called the Shao Lin Temple. The achievements of the Shao Lin system made it the most popular style while also earning for Chinese Wu Su respect and dignity. Because of the revered status of the Shao Lin system and the fact that most modern styles find their ancestry in the Shao Lin Temple, the history of this style will receive primary emphasis. The following information was found in the *Wu Tan Journal* (Chinese edition) and from several pieces of informal history.

The first Shao Lin Temple was built in 377 A.D. on Shao Shih Mountain, Teng Fon Hsien, Huo Nan province by order of Emperor Wei. The Emperor built the temple for a Buddhist named Pao Jaco for the purpose of preaching and worship; at this time no martial art training was done by the monks. In 527 A.D. during the Liang dynasty a Buddhist prince, Da Mo (Figure 1), of an Indian tribe, came to the temple for religious preaching. But when Da Mo came, he saw that many of the monks were sick and weak. In order to find a way to strengthen the monks, Da Mo locked himself in a room for nine years of meditation; when Da Mo came out he wrote his results down in two books: *Shi Sui Ching* and *Yi Gin Ching*. Da Mo died in 539 A.D.

The *Shi Sui Ching* was primarily a religious treatise explaining methods for the cultivation of the Buddhist spirit, while the *Yi Gin Ching* taught ways to strengthen the physical body. Unfortunately, after a few generations, the contents of the first book were lost. They were lost probably because few people practiced its hard methods and principles. However, the *Yi Gin Ching* was taught in the Shao Lin Temple for generations to increase external muscular power and also to increase what is referred to as internal power (see the section on "Common Knowledge").

The increase in external and internal power encouraged the monks to investigate its special properties and characteristics in order to develop ways to apply it for self-defense against thieves and robbers. The necessity of protecting themselves against criminals was especially vital since many monks travelled far from their temples to preach and help people. Consequently, the learning of martial technique became a required course of study in addition to religious studies. It must be remembered that the monks spent more time in the study of Buddhism and spiritual cultivation than on martial arts.

Unfortunately, thirty years after Da Mo's death, a few monks with weak morals left the temple and roamed the countryside robbing and killing. Because of their martial technique and power, ordinary people were defenseless. As a result, the Emperor (Chou dynasty, 570 A.D.) ordered the temple to close down. It wasn't until thirty years after the closing of the temple and a new dynasty, the Sui (600 A.D.), that the Shao Lin Temple was allowed to resume its activities. To avoid any more occurences of immoral and unscrupulous behavior, strict guidelines for moral education were instituted. The teaching of martial technique and morality went hand-in-hand.

From 600 to 1600 A.D., the martial arts through the Shao Lin Temple grew into the most complete system of Wu Su in China and in the rest of the world. During this period, the Shao Lin monks researched and developed internal power, external power, medita-

菩提達摩祖師

Figure 1

tion, various barehand and weapon techniques, massage, herbal remedies, etc. The Shao Lin system soon came to be recognized as the authoritative way of Wu Su. In this period more than ten Shao Lin Temples were built. Moreover, especially during the Ming dynasty (1368–1644), the monks and their system were also viewed as agents for virtue and justice. Everywhere a Shao Lin monk went, his martial ability was always used to help and protect people.

The Shao Lin way became so influential that it even spread to Japan, Korea, and other parts of Indo-China. The oldest martial art recorded in Japan is described as the "seizing technique of Ming's people" or the "soft technique." This soft technique was taught by a Chinese monk named Chen Yuan-Yen, who spent his life in Japan during the Ming dynasty. Chen's soft technique later developed into the "soft way" or *Judo.*

In 1644 disaster struck the Chinese people and the Shao Lin Temple. In that year the Manchurians invaded and conquered China, thus starting the Chin dynasty. In order to consolidate their control, the Manchurians began to destroy the largest martial arts organization in China: the Shao Lin Temple. Two hundred years of murder and destruction followed the invasion of the Manchus. Around 1760, a massive attack was launched against the Shao Lin monks which resulted in many deaths and in many temples being burned. Some monks were forced to hide among the people or flee to Japan and Korea. Never again was the Shao Lin Temple to regain its greatness.

With the dispersion of the Shao Lin monks and the destruction of their temple it became impossible to train new monks in Wu Su. However, the monks who were hiding began to teach the people their system. The teaching of Wu Su to non-Shao-Lin monks became widespread and eventually led to the creation of many modern styles.

It is interesting to note that although Shao Lin monks were educated in a common system, there still developed different styles among their students. The reason for this may be traced to the training procedure of the Shao Lin monks. Every monk was required to pass through ten separate stages of training, each of which emphasized a different aspect of Wu Su. After the monks completed the stages they were required to specialize in one or two stages; so when the monks taught ordinary people, they naturally put more emphasis on their specialty. As time progressed, the divisions became more separated. Furthermore, because students who were learning a certain specialty had no contact with others who were also learning the same specialty, there occured a tendency for one division to split into separate styles.

Many of the monks, however, did more than teach Wu Su to ordinary people—they and their disciples organized resistance movements against the Chin dynasty. The reestablishment of the previous Ming dynasty became the goal of many Chinese. To symbolize the wish to return to the glory of the Ming, Shao Lin disciples used a special hand signal—this hand signal is seen in Figure 2. In Chinese the word *Ming* means "bright" and is composed of the characters for the sun and the moon, the two great sources of light or brightness. The right hand in a fist symbolized the sun and the left open hand symbolized the moon; together the fist and open hand meant bright or Ming. When a person showed the hand signal he indicated two things: first, the Ming dynasty must return, and secondly, that the person showing the hand signal was himself "bright" and an agent for justice. In Figure 3 is shown the written Buddhist symbol; this is also a very common, centuries old symbol used by many earlier Buddhists. This symbol (read *Won*) is an old Indian Buddhist mystic emblem which means "good fortune and virtue."

Even though the Shao Lin Temple was never to regain its former greatness, it did begin to resume some activity around the 1800s. Two main causes contributed to the resurgence of the Temple: internal Chin corruption and external invasions by Western powers. At the turn of the 18th century, corruption was wide spread in the Chin dynasty;

Figure 2

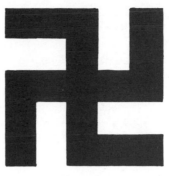

Figure 3

as a result, the regime was weak in enforcing its rule. Added to this was the military and economic invasion of China by the Western powers of England, France, and Russia. The Chin was forced to spend so many of its resources in the fight against the Westerners that the Shao Lin Temple was able to operate with some freedom.

In addition, there were some other minor causes which helped the Shao Lin Temple to resume activity. Around 1860 the Chin army first began to use the gun on a wide scale. With the gun at their disposal, the Chin rulers had a tremendous advantage over the monks. By thus possessing the gun, the Chin authorities felt confident in their ability to overcome the monks at any time.

A second minor factor which allowed the Shao Lin monks to resume activity was the inability of the temple to achieve its former greatness. Because of the previous persecution, the Shao Lin Temple lost many monks who were outstanding and knowledgeable martial artists; the total loss was irreparable. While the Shao Lin system was still the best martial organization in China, producing many good martial artists, it was nevertheless not as great as in previous generations. Due to its diminished state, the Chin rulers felt that the Shao Lin system posed no major threat to their safety. Another factor which reinforced this was the fact that the Chinese people began to ignore the study and practice of martial arts; fewer people were willing to devote themselves to the ancient study.

Finally, in 1911, the Chinese people ended the tyranny of the Chin dynasty by a revolution lead by Dr. Sun Yet-Sen. After the revolution, seventeen years of civil war occurred before the country was reunited. But during the reunification of the country, the Shao Lin Temple was to receive its final tragedy. The final tragedy began in 1926.

In that year Chiang Kai-Shek began the reunification of China by launching the now famous Northern Expedition (1926–1928). The purpose of the Northern Expedition was to rid the country of the numerous warlords who stood in the way of a united China. To accomplish this purpose in Huo Nan province, the home of the main Shao Lin Temple, Chiang Kai-Shek appointed General Fong Yu-Hsiang to fight the warlord Farn Chung-Shiow.

The attack on Farn Chung-Shiow was, in the end, to prove fatal for the Shao Lin Temple. It seems that at the time of Fong's offensive, commanded in the field by his lieutenant, Shih Yeou-Shan, the warlord Farn was intimate friends with Meaw Shing, the Fan Jang or Head Master of the main Shao Lin Temple. (Meaw Shing himself was an extraordinary monk who was proficient in martial arts and in other things such as classical literature. But Meaw Shing was also vain in his passion for wanting to associate with important people; his vanity led him to befriend Farn Chung-Shiow.) When Shih's troops routed Farn's army, Farn was forced to flee. Farn eventually fled to the Shao Lin Temple where he received protection from Meaw Shing.

To protect Farn, Meaw Shing ordered the Shao Lin monks to fight against Shih's troops. While the monks were good fighters, the superior arms of Shih's troops overcame them. When victory came the soldiers were so enraged by the action of Meaw Shing that they burned the Shao Lin Temple. Meaw Shing died in this battle. This terrible action in 1927 was the final burning of the Shao Lin Temple.

During the period that the Shao Lin Temple was active in this century, there arose in Shanghai a famous martial organization which has spread to various parts of Asia. In March of 1909, Huo Yuen-Jar, Figure 4, who was taught Mi Zoun Chuan by his father, Huo Ien-Di, arrived in Shanghai from Tientsin and founded the Chin Woo Association. But in August of the same year Huo Yuen-Jar was poisoned to death. Undaunted by the death, the followers of Huo Yuen-Jar kept up his spirit and continued to operate the Chin Woo Association by inviting such famous masters as Chen Zhih-Zeng (Eagle Division), Lo Kuan-Yu (Northern Praying Mantis Division), Geeng Cia-Kuan (Hsing Yi Division), and Wu Chien-Chuan who founded the Wu style of Tai Chi Chuan. Although the Chin Woo Association closed down during World War II, it eventually reopened and today there are 16 branches in various parts of Asia which includes the one founded in Hong Kong in 1918.

Once the country was finally united, the government began an active program to revitalize and reorganize Wu Su. In 1928, in Nan King, the Nan King Central Kuo Su Institute was founded for the purpose of consolidating Wu Su by bringing great masters together under one formal organization, with Chang Chih-Chiang (Figure 5) as its first director. Since that time, Wu Su has been referred to as Kuo Su, which means "national technique." The masters who were invited included Gu Zou-Chang, Won Lai-Shen, Fu Chan-Song, Wong Shao-Chou, and Li Shan-Wu. They specialized in North Shao Lin Nature Division, Pa Gua Division, Li Far Spear and Tan Twe Division, respectively. These men were particularly known as the Five Northern Tigers. Also influencing the Central Kuo Su Institute were Geeng Dar-Hai (Ta Chan Division), Don Ien-Gieh (Yang's Tai Chi Chuan) and Shun Yu-Fon (Lo Han Division). The Chin Woo masters that were previously mentioned also greatly influenced the Central Kuo Su Institute course of instruction. These masters rose to the occasion and overcame age-old prejudices to discuss side-by-side the best techniques of each division. For this reason the style that developed at the Central Kuo Su Institute contains elements from many divisions. This diverse style has come to be popularly known as Long Fist. In a few years this organization had earned a great reputation.

Later the Five Northern Tigers were sent to Canton to help General Li Zen-Chao to organize another Kuo Su Institute. This time at the Institute in Canton famous Southern division masters were invited to attend. They included Lin In-Tan (Mou Cah Chuan Division), Tan Shan (Chai Li Fou Division), Lin Yaw-Kuai (Dragon Style Division), Chang Li-Chuan (White Brow Division), Lin Shih-Zon (Hung Gar Division), and Wu Gsao-Jon (White Crane Division). At this new Central Kuo Su Institute Northern and Southern styles were mixed, forming new and effective techniques.

In 1937 disaster struck again with the invasion of the Japanese, thus starting World War II. The Central Institute was closed with many of its members joining the resistance against the Japanese. During the eight long years of war, many masters and students were killed while others taught and studied whenever they could. It was during this time that author Yang's third Master,* Li Mao-Ching, began his training.

---

* Si Fu is the traditional Chinese word for "master;" it means "teacher" and "father." Other important relationship titles in Chinese Wu Su are Tuo Di which means "disciple" and "brother," Si Shon which means "teacher" and "older brother," and Si Di which means "teacher" and "younger brother." The Si Fu will refer to all his students as Tuo Di while the students will refer to each other as Si Shon or Si Di depending on whether the classmate is older or younger in terms of experience.

Figure 4   Figure 5

After the Communist take-over of mainland China in 1949, many Wu Su masters left for Hong Kong or Taiwan where they could practice their art in greater freedom. During the exodus from mainland China a new generation of Wu Su instructors took up the responsibility for teaching Wu Su: Li Mao-Ching is of this generation of instructors. Master Li Mao-Ching's main instructor, Han Ching-Tan (1903–1976), was a second generation martial artist in the Central Kuo Su Institute. Master Li also studied under the Northern Praying Mantis and Chinese wrestling expert Fu Jar-Bin (1914–) and studied Sun Bin Chuan under Kao Fan-Shien (1914–).

There is much more to tell of the history of Chinese Kung Fu, but it is hoped that this short history will give a general idea as to the main development of Wu Su. Many styles exist today with a diversity of theory and technique; even though the styles are different, each in its own way is carrying on the great tradition of the original Shao Lin system. In the later volumes of this set on Long Fist there will be informal histories about some of the Northern styles because Long Fist itself is integrally related and derived from many Northern divisions.

MORALITY

In Chinese society it is common for parents to send their children to receive formal training in martial arts. For the Western parent this may seem unusual because they think of martial arts as somehow encouraging violence. But for the Chinese parent the exact opposite is true; martial arts is a way to train the child in good habits of mind and body. The Chinese community in general, and Chinese martial society in particular, have always believed morality to be an integral part of Wu Su.

To understand the proper relation of morality to Kung Fu, two important points must be introduced. The first, and the most important, fact in Kung Fu is that the level of achievement of any martial artist is directly dependent on his morality. If the martial artist is a bad person, then his ability can only reach certain limited levels; if the martial artist is a good person, then there is no real limit to what he can achieve.

This idea is admittedly strange to many Westerners. In the West an athlete such as a football or baseball player may be a heavy drinker, take drugs, engage in malicious actions and act immaturely, and yet it is believed that such overall behavior will in no way reflect on the athlete's actual or potential abilities. The Chinese martial artist obviously does not subscribe to this philosophy.

The second point relates to the defining of morality. Some people hold the notion that morality is merely restricted to restraining themselves from stealing, lying, cheating, and other negative acts. For the Chinese martial artist such simple restraints are not enough. Morality for the Kung Fu practitioner is a *total* way of *acting* and *thinking;* morality, as a condition of life, is lived every second in thought and deed. If the martial artist is working, talking, playing, eating, or doing a thousand other activities, his way of being or morality is constantly a part of his character. In the actual training and mechanics of morality two categories are taught to every student; the morality of action and the morality of mind. These categories reflect the dual development of deed and thought.

The morality of action may be defined as how the martial artist should behave outwardly to the world. Five important traits compose the morality of action: they are humility, respect, righteousness, trust, and loyalty. The student should commit these ideals to memory. At this point let us begin with humility.

In China there is a saying, "humility gains and pride loses." When a person is humble he admits, in a sense, that there exists something above him, or at the moment something beyond his reach. This attitude when closely examined is the foundation for all learning. If a student felt adequate and satisfied (pride) with what he had learned, then the ability to reach out beyond his scope would be destroyed. By being humble, the martial artist realizes that what he knows is next to nothing; there is always a gap to fill in by constant learning and practice. In this way "humility gains" by instilling in the martial artist the understanding that he is incomplete in his ability and thus must keep striving for perfection. The final outcome is a better martial artist in mind and ability.

From the above it is easy to see why "pride loses." Pride creates a feeling of satisfaction and adequacy. A mental block is created by giving the martial artist a false sense of achievement. The result is that growth and ability come to a halt. If the martial artist thinks he is good, then why should he practice as hard? If he isn't humble, there is no way to improve and reach high levels of ability; morality goes hand-in-hand with achievement.

Respect is intimately related to humility. If a person has humility it is easy to give respect because both traits involve the recognition of goodness in everything. Respect occupies a special position in the relationship between martial artists of all styles. By giving respect, dignity is gained for all martial styles. Respect and dignity give martial arts an importance beyond words; every person from the instructor to the beginning student realizes through respect that martial arts is not mere fighting, but something that strives for pure spirit. In this way respect for and obedience to the master become absolutely imperative, since it is the master who will be the guide to the higher levels of ability and spirituality.

Loyalty, righteousness, and trust complete the traits of morality of action. When the martial artist has righteousness he will stand up for justice and fight evil whenever he can; to fully complement these actions the martial artist must also have a good approach to life. Having trust means not that the martial artist will trust everybody, but that everybody can trust the martial artist. By showing his dependability and honesty, the student shows other people that his character will be guided by goodness.

Loyalty involves faithfulness to the ideals of family, culture, nation, and martial style. In particular, a student may someday be called upon to teach his particular style, which he must honor by teaching what he has learned to be the traditional aspects of his style. Without this loyalty, a style will undergo as many changes as there are instructors; in time the established forms which have been proven effective and which have identified the style through the ages will disappear. The death of the style will surely come about if this happens. There is always room for innovation, but innovation must occur within the context of an established tradition.

The second aspect of morality, the morality of mind, also has five major traits. They are: will, endurance, perseverance, patience, and bravery. Morality of mind, as contrasted to the morality of action, deals with the inward spirit or soul of the martial artist. Will, of all the traits, is the center point.

In China there is a saying, "If a man is a ship, then the will is his rudder." The martial artist must have something which stands determined to control and direct his energies. It is easy to say that everybody should have a strong will, but for the martial artist it is particularly important. For nearly all of his life, the true martial artist will devote at least three hours of every day for practice; only a strong will can push the martial artist to make this tremendous sacrifice. The will grows in importance once the student realizes that the study of martial arts is a lifetime commitment. Martial arts should not be a hobby which a person drops after a few months or years of practice. Devotion to a lifetime of martial arts requires a guiding force during the times of personal trouble, sadness, laziness, and self-doubt—only the will can provide such a force.

The other traits can be thought of as supporting the will. Endurance can be likened to the physical fuel or energy source of the will. If the body engages in difficult exercises or if the person is tired and sore, then it is endurance which keeps the body whole. If endurance is the physical fuel of will then perseverance and patience are the mental sources of energy for the will. In performing difficult tasks the mental as well as the physical side is affected; when the mind is in pain or is exhausted then perseverance and patience must be present. Sometimes weeks, months, and years of practice are required to perfect certain techniques; during these times the martial artist must never get discouraged. By having perseverance and patience the student will endure.

Lastly, bravery can be seen as the principle of action for the will. Bravery for the martial artist is the spiritual courage needed to face the truth. In facing the truth the martial artist must stand up to any situation and deal with it in an honest and courageous way. The martial artist will always meet the challenges of life head on whether in failure or in success. Secondly, bravery involves the courage to fight evil as the Shao Lin monks once fought evil. The martial artist must follow the example of the Shao Lin Temple and become an active agent for the establishment of justice and righteousness; if the principles of the Shao Lin monk can be followed, then the martial artist can make this world a much better place.

Many more points can be made about martial morality, but as the student makes each trait a part of his character he will find that some things become obvious. As an example, once humility becomes a living ideal the thought of showing off or being boisterous disappears. The martial artist will realize that showing off and boasting are the disguises of pride and limited martial ability.

In explaining and teaching morality, a device commonly used by many masters to make the lesson more clear is the anecdote or story. The anecdotes are usually fanciful tales that entertain while they teach the student valuable points on the proper conduct of a martial artist. To make the previous discussion on morality more vivid and alive, two well known stories will be presented to illustrate some important aspects of martial conduct.

STORY 1

During the early years of the Chin dynasty two brothers lived near Jeou Lien Mountain, Pu Zon Hsien of Fu Chien province. Ever since the time of their early youth the older brother, who was bigger and stronger, constantly oppressed the younger, weaker, brother. Rarely did a day pass which did not see the older brother intimidate the younger. This situation was especially made worse by the death of their father.

When the father died he split his land in half and gave an equal portion to each brother. But the older brother, not fearing the authority of his father anymore, decided to take away his weaker brother's rightful inheritance. To take away anyone's land was at that time a great tragedy because a person's whole livelihood depended on the amount of land he had to cultivate. Everyday the older brother took a little land away from his brother; after a few months the younger brother found that he had no more land left. Utterly discouraged he was forced to move out.

For weeks the younger brother attempted to regain his land by bargaining, asking relatives to interfere, and seeking help from the authorities; all of the methods failed. Finally, the younger brother concluded that he had to build up his own body while learning martial arts—only violence could force his brother to give back his inheritance. To achieve this, the younger brother travelled to the greatest of all martial schools—the Shao Lin Temple. The younger brother did not have to go far because a division of the famous Shao Lin Temple was located in Jeou Lien Mountain.

Upon entering the temple he sought the master of the Shao Lin monks to ask for martial training. "Master," he said humbly, "I have come to the Shao Lin Temple to ask a great favor from you."

"Ask and I shall attempt to honor your request," replied the master.

"With your permission, I will gather water, plow the land, scrub the temple walls, and cook meals in the great kitchen if you will teach me martial arts."

"But why do you wish to learn?"

"So I can get my rightful inheritance back from my brother. He has taken all the land my father left for me. I tried every peaceful path to get it back. Now, only violence is the answer."

Without hesitation the master answered, "Yes."

Word soon spread about the younger brother and his request. Many people who heard the story wondered at the reasoning of the master; some people could not believe that a Shao Lin monk would teach someone martial arts with the intention of purposeful violence. But those who understood the ways and habits of the Shao Lin monks knew that the younger brother would get a valuable lesson from his training.

To begin training the younger brother, the master found a small young willow tree and asked the brother to jump over the tree while holding a new born calf, which was given to the younger brother as a present by the master. The younger brother was commanded to do this task everyday, to jump over the same willow tree while holding the same calf. As time passed, the quick growing willow became taller and the calf grew bigger and heavier. After three years of this task, the younger brother was able to jump the tall willow with a cow in his hands.

After the third year, the younger brother soon became impatient with this task and went to see the master. "Master, for three years I have been jumping over the willow with the cow and I still haven't learned the techniques of fighting. When will I begin to learn these things?"

The master, with a smile on his face, answered, "Young man, your training is now over. You now possess the ability to get back your rightful inheritance. Take the cow that you have been training with and go back to your land and start ploughing it."

"But," the brother replied, "what will I do when my older brother comes to force me out?"

"Pick up the cow and run toward your brother," answered the master.

The younger brother was utterly shocked by this statement. He pleaded with the master, but the master insisted he was now capable of his original goal. The younger brother left the Shao Lin Temple very disappointed. But still, he decided to do what the monk advised. He was hoping that his brother had changed in the three years since his absence.

The younger brother soon arrived home and began immediately to plow the land with the cow with which he had practiced for three years. The older brother quickly appeared and said, "Brother, do you think that you can get your land back? Never! Now get off this land before I beat you." The younger brother immediately picked up his cow and ran towards his brother. The older brother was so amazed and shocked at this feat that he ran away and never returned. The younger brother at last regained his rightful inheritance and more—his dignity and respect.

Imaginative stories like this one are often used to point out a moral which will teach the martial student the meaning of the Shao Lin spirit. This story in particular tries to stress two major points. First, Kung Fu is meant only for self-defense—not for premeditated violence against others. The younger brother eventually got what he wanted without violence.

Second, the story points out that the learning of Kung Fu requires patience and constant repetition or practice. To spend three years to achieve proficiency in his technique the younger brother needed patience. Added to this was the need to constantly practice. But in showing the constant practice that the younger brother performed, the story also showed that progressive resistance is required. Over a period of time the student must have greater and greater resistance to overcome. Each day that the younger brother practiced, the height of the willow and the weight of the cow increased by a small amount. By slowly going to higher stages the younger brother achieved his goal.

STORY 2

In ancient times, if a youngster wished to learn Kung Fu he would have to pledge himself to a master. This pledge involved certain duties for the student and master. One of the most important parts of this pledge was the promise the student made not to leave his master without having perfected and finished all the requirements set down for the style. This promise was made for two reasons. First, if a student left prematurely and was unable to defend himself against other martial artists, then the master's reputation would suffer. People would think the master was bad because his students were bad. Second, this pledge kept students from revealing the secrets of the style.

Some ancient masters were particularly strict in enforcing the rule against premature leave-taking. A few masters went so far as to kill the runaway students. Although the killings were never justified, many people accepted the situation and let the masters do what they wanted.

Although the penalties could be severe in ancient times for a runaway student, there exists a popular story about how one student did try to escape. In Northern China, there lived a boy who pledged himself to a famous local master. When the boy entered the master's school, he soon found that the training was hard and the master paid little attention to him. In fact, the early years with this master were spent in serving him and the student's older classmates. But the student persevered and learned by watching the master and older classmates; after watching he would constantly imitate and practice the forms and techniques.

Years passed and still the master barely noticed or taught the student. All during this time the student kept up his watching and practicing. The student became disenchanted with his master's apparent lack of concern; he made up his mind to run away. The student understood and feared the consequences of his action, so he began to plan in advance. The fateful day quickly arrived. But unknown to the student, his master had discovered the escape plan. The master decided that he would invite the student to dinner and test him; if the student failed the special test, then he would be discreetly killed.

During the dinner, the master put a hard pea in his mouth and spit the pea at him. This particular master was very famous for being able to use internal and external power when spitting anything out of his mouth. Spitting can be very effective and dangerous in fighting, especially if a martial artist can spit out any hard object he previously put in his mouth; if such projectiles were to strike the eye or vital cavities of the face, great damage could result.

So when the master spit the pea at him, the student instantly knew that his master was trying to hurt him. Without thinking the student moved his chopsticks and caught the pea in midair; the student's continuous practice had given him fast enough reactions to catch the pea. The amazed master saw this and said, "I had never realized that you have such a capability to defend yourself. I can teach you no more; you are free to go at any time." The student suddenly realized that his time and training were not in vain; feeling very sorry the student threw himself on the floor and asked that his master forgive him and take him back as a student.

This popular story illustrates several important points. It is not uncommon for a master to ignore many students. He does it not out of cold heartedness, but because he wants to test the student in order to find out if that student cares enough about martial arts; the student in essence must prove his interest and patience. The students who will eventually be taught the most hidden secrets must show that they are worthy of the trust.

Secondly, this story pointed out the nature or final outcome of Kung Fu training. Although the student was never specially trained to catch objects with a pair of chopsticks, he was able to do it. This type of spontaneous and unrehearsed action only comes about by practicing live techniques; because the student was so serious and diligent in his practice, he developed concentration and reaction. Concentration and reaction lead, in a way, to the ultimate aim of any Chinese martial artist: to act in any situation quickly, naturally, and without thinking.

In conclusion, it becomes clear that morality and martial arts must go together. As a person improves in martial ability, he should also improve in his ways of thinking and acting. As a closing to this section the authors would like to leave the reader these Chinese proverbs to enjoy and ponder:

"There is a sky above a sky, and a talent above a talent."

"The more bamboo grows the lower it bows."

"The half-filled water bucket makes great splashing noises; the full bucket is silent."

COMMON KNOWLEDGE

In Wu Su there exists a certain set of principles which are shared by every division. Although each division has evolved different methods to achieve certain goals, the principles behind the methods are nevertheless the same. This foundation of commonly shared principles helps to unite Kung Fu artists regardless of style. For this reason these principles shall be referred to as Wu Su's common knowledge. For the beginning student this section will be necessary reading before starting the later chapters. For the experienced

Wu Su practitioner some parts will be a review, while other sections may offer new information about old concepts. The general reader may find this section extremely helpful in giving him a wide introduction to many misunderstood principles of Wu Su which are held by the non-martial public.

Wu Su Styles in China

Westerners who seek to learn an Eastern martial art are many times confused and bewildered because of the vast number of styles that are in existence; in particular, Chinese Kung Fu has within its own sphere a number of different divisions and subdivisions. In order to sort out the relationship among Kung Fu styles, it is first necessary to get a broad geographical background.

To start, it can be seen that important countries close to China have their own particular martial styles. Well known examples of these local styles can be seen in Japanese Karate and Korean Tae Kwan Do. Even though these countries near China have their own martial systems, Chinese Wu Su as a whole has been the major influence in the origin and development of many important Eastern styles. For example, Karate is thought to have originated with Shao Lin monks and other Chinese emissaries who travelled to Japan for various religious, cultural, and economic reasons*. This type of influence was not unusual at the time because many underdeveloped countries around China actively sought to incorporate as many aspects of Chinese culture as possible.

Turning to China itself, the relationship of styles can be based on geography. The major geographical dividing line is the Yellow River, which divides Wu Su styles into Northern and Southern divisions. Although the overwhelming majority of styles are either Northern or Southern, a small number are not classified according to this system. In particular, the Mongolian (Northern China) and Tibetan or La Ma** (Western China) are not classified as Northern or Southern division.

By dividing Wu Su into Northern and Southern divisions, a functional as well as a geographical distinction is made. Northern styles usually emphasize leg or kicking techniques with the middle and long range attack (see "Fundamental Stances" in Chapter 2 for a definition of middle and long range). It is thought that the Northern divisions developed kicking and the long and middle range attack because the Chinese people in the North were generally taller and had longer legs. Taking advantage of the height difference, the Northern styles naturally developed techniques which suited their longer arms and legs. Though the Northern divisions do have hand techniques, they are usually geared for the long punch or strike. Examples of some Northern styles are Long Fist, Ta Shan Pi Kwa, Cha Chuan, Lo Han, Eagle Claw, and Northern Praying Mantis.

Because the Southern Chinese were shorter than the Northern people, they developed hand techniques for the middle and short range. The Southern divisions do have kicks, but they are less in number and variety than the Northern styles; although quite naturally, the Southern styles have a greater number and variety of hand techniques. A further distinction between Southern and Northern styles is the lowness of stances. The Southern style's stances are much lower than the Northern styles. Practitioners of Southern styles move and use their hands and legs in very low stances while practitioners of Northern styles must stand high for their type of long range attack. The Southern division includes White Crane, Mou Cha, Chai Li Fou, Dragon, Hung Gar, White Brow, Monkey, Tiger, Southern Praying Mantis, and Wing Chun.

---

*For a good overview of Eastern martial history see Bruce Haines, *Karate's History and Traditions*, C. E. Tuttle, 1968.
**La Ma division, which is related to White Crane, is sometimes classified as a Southern division by some martial artists.

Wu Su styles may also be classified on the basis of whether a style is *internal* or *external* in its emphasis. If a style is internal, then the cultivation of *Chi* and internal power (refer to "Chi" in this section) is given priority over external technique. When internal power is adequately developed, then external technique will be given emphasis. The mastery of an internal division takes many years because the first prerequisite is the smooth circulation of Chi through the entire body. This process by itself usually takes ten years. An added barrier to the mastery of an internal division is the scarcity of competent masters. The time and patience needed to reach adequate levels is so great that few people have been able to achieve competency. The internal divisions were developed in Central China and include Tai Chi, Hsing Yi, Pa Kwa, and Lieu Huo Ba Far.

In the past, the original purpose for learning an internal division was self-defense, but in modern times this purpose has changed. Currently, people who practice Tai Chi Chuan, Hsing Yi, or some other internal style, are interested in the health or physical fitness aspect of the system. Through years of research, Chinese martial artists have found that by practicing the methods which help the circulation of Chi they also gained improved health; improved health may be the better functioning of the internal organs such as the heart, lungs, kidneys, and stomach, and the curing of high blood pressure, arthritis, and ulcers.

The external divisions, in contrast to the internal, emphasize external technique and muscle power before internal Chi power. The external divisions will develop kicking, blocking, punching, dodging, etc. before moving on to the development of internal power. The mastery of an external division usually does not take as long as that of an internal division because the outer techniques are easier to practice and develop. All of the Northern and Southern divisions previously mentioned are examples of external Kung Fu.

Basic Concepts in Wu Su

For Chinese martial artists the practice and mastery of a technique is second only to the cultivation of morality. To understand the idea of a technique it is necessary to start with the concept of a "form" (*Shih*). A form is any single block, kick, dodge, jump, grasp, punch, etc. by itself; an example of a form is a heel kick or a backward jump. Every form has been developed so that it achieves a maximum of speed and power with a minimum of danger for the person performing the form. Many forms were invented in imitation of such animals as the crane, monkey, or tiger. The invention of new forms does not negate the traditional forms, but if the inventor is ignorant of basic principles, he may create a useless and dangerous form.

A "technique" (*Dsao*), then, can be a single form or any number of combined forms used in specific situations for the purpose of defense or attack. For example, some techniques may employ only one form such as a block or punch while others are special combinations such as a block and punch. Techniques which use two forms usually have a defensive form such as a blocking or dodging maneuver along with an attack form such as a kick. In addition, some techniques may use three or four forms against certain types of attacks. Sometimes one of the forms may be a fake to trap the opponent.

Every technique also has what is called a solution. If an opponent starts a certain action such as a punch to the face he sets up a problem for the martial artist. The technique, then, becomes the particular solution to a particular problem; in other words, the solution is the use of the technique. As an example, a punch to the face may be solved by a technique composed of a circular block and a kick to the opponent's knee (although this is not the only technique that can solve the problem); the martial artist can then apply this solution any time a punch is thrown to his face. In addition, one technique may hide two or three solutions—this aspect is treated in Chapter 5.

Solutions are very important because they define the special use of the technique. A student may know the motions of the technique, but if he does not know its solution then he cannot apply the technique. In fact, some masters only teach the outward motions of the technique and teach the solutions when they feel the student has sufficient moral training.

To practice techniques, Chinese martial artists take from ten to thirty offensive or defensive techniques and perform them in a continuous flowing routine called a Tan (sequence). In English this word is also translated as set or forms; the authors prefer to use the term "sequence" since this word describes more accurately the essence of a Tan. The value of the sequences cannot be overestimated because they lie at the heart of the learning, practicing, and perfecting of every style's techniques.

Every authentic Wu Su style will have its own sequences which contain techniques particular to that style. The sequences of any style are its way of keeping the history and experience of the style alive; sequences become all the more precious since they hold thousands of years of research and investigation. To neglect and cast aside the practice of established sequences is to throw away the practical knowledge of past generations.

In practicing a sequence, a student seeks to increase the reaction, speed, and power of the techniques. By constantly practicing a sequence the student begins to make each technique a part of his second nature. Once the second nature has been developed he can then apply each technique automatically and smoothly. In fact, one of the prerequisites for free fighting is the ability to perform certain sequences at competent levels. Every time a student practices a sequence he is also practicing his stability because of the constant movement and changing of stances. Usually the student must practice a sequence a thousand times before he can remember it for life and approach adequate levels of speed and power.

In Chinese Wu Su there exists a wide variety of sequences ranging from the simple to the most complex. Included are barehanded sequences, weapon sequences for wide and narrow blade swords, rod sequences, two short rod sequences, spear sequences, and many more. The creation of new sequences is not discouraged, but only those who have a solid Wu Su background should attempt this.

Although sequences are extremely important, some misinformed martial artists believe that sequences are beautiful, yet useless, forms of dancing. They believe that sequences are impractical. Those who believe this know very little about Chinese Kung Fu. The techniques in every sequence are there because they are practical methods of defense or attack.

Once a student has mastered the techniques from the sequences, he must start learning how to apply those techniques with reaction, speed, accuracy, and power. The eventual goal is to use the techniques within the sequences for free fighting. To start the training for free fighting the student will begin with fighting forms. In China a fighting form is called Twe Sou or Twe Shih which means "opposing hands" or "opposing form." Fighting forms are pre-set patterns in which two or three students practice one, two, or three techniques in a continuous fashion. By continuously practicing a few techniques, the student builds up an automatic reaction to certain situations.

When the student has gained enough proficiency and reaction through the fighting forms, he will move into the practice of a two-man or three-man fighting sequence. In China a fighting sequence is called Twe Tan or Twe Tse. The fighting sequence usually has ten to thirty techniques which the students practice in a continuous motion. The purpose of a fighting sequence is to put the student, as closely as possible, in a situation that resembles free fighting. By doing this the student trains those traits which are vitally important for unrestricted fighting. Even though the techniques in the fighting sequence are pre-set, each student must execute every offensive and defensive technique with quick reaction, power, and speed. The fighting sequence is not a mere dance; it is an actual, full scale, yet controlled fight in which each side uses the maximum amount of speed and power. The final stage is to fight using no set patterns—this last stage is *Sun Sou*, which means "free fighting."

Wu Su Training

In the process of training that goes into the making of a Chinese martial artist, the first step is to pick a good master. Chinese martial artists have a saying, "It is better to spend three years looking for a good master than to spend ten years with a bad one."

In America the problem of picking a good master is particularly difficult because few instructors have had traditional training. Many instructors pass themselves off as teachers of Kung Fu when in fact they are not teaching Chinese Wu Su, but another martial style.

With any master the history of his training is very important. It is not so important what style a person has learned, but the number of years he has studied and practiced the style. The age of the master is not necessarily important because many young masters began their training as children. In Chinese Kung Fu there are no two-year masters or ninety day wonders. If possible, the beginning student should seek out the person who taught the instructor. Good masters produce good students, and good students make good masters. Beware of masters who claim to be experts in a number of different styles. Many of these instructors only spend a short time studying a style and then claim they are experts.

In actually observing a master at work, the student should look for several important points. Is the master's morality good? Does he have a good training schedule? Does he adequately explain the tradition and history of his style? Is the master stable, smooth, quick, and protective of vital areas while performing? When the master explains sequences or techniques do his explanations seem reasonable? In looking for these characteristics the student should be able to eliminate many bad instructors. The masters who are left should again be studied applying the same criteria as before. If the beginning student keeps his eyes and ears open, he should be able to pick a good master.

After picking the master, the student will find that in Chinese Wu Su the general program of training is remarkably the same for all divisions. The traits necessary to be a good martial artist are the same regardless of the style. The first part of any training will usually entail moral instruction and the learning of a few techniques. In the way of techniques the student is taught fundamental stances and a few defensive moving forms. The work at this time is simple but extremely hard. It is usual for the students who are not perseverant to abandon Wu Su training at this time.

It is very important that beginning students at this time lay a firm foundation in their training of stability. Without stability the martial artist's speed, power, and coordination of techniques cannot go beyond simple levels. Stability is usually judged on the lowness of stances or a low center of gravity. Still, a martial artist should not stand so low that his freedom of movement is impaired.

The importance of stability can be readily seen during some martial arts tournaments. During these tournaments it is fairly common for a person to fall while sparring. In a real fight, falling down is probably the worst thing that can happen. The person is then vulnerable to any attack. Falling down is usually due to a lack of stability which results from overly high stances. The single greatest influence on the belief that high stances are effective is the martial art movie. Although the movies may show "great" techniques, one still should remember that it is all make-believe. In traditional Chinese Wu Su, low stances are extremely important.

A drill which at this time fully symbolizes the first six months of practice is Ma Bu training (see Chapter 2 for the Ma Bu stance). There are two purposes to Ma Bu training: first, by standing in the Ma Bu stance from five to ten minutes, the student is building up the stability and power of his legs, and second, because Ma Bu training is long and hard, it trains the patience and the endurance of the student. Getting through Ma Bu training indicates to the master that the student may have the proper mental attitude necessary to be a martial artist.

At this point it would be interesting to see how the Shao Lin monks trained their novices for stability and patience. Shao Lin temples were usually located on the sides of mountains near river valleys; therefore, in order to obtain water the novices had to be sent down to the river. But on the route to the river the monks required the novices to use only prearranged tree stumps which were on the path (years earlier the monks had planted the trees and later cut them to stumps).

As the novices went to get water, they were required to jump or walk from stump to stump. By jumping from stump to stump, the buckets began to swing; the swinging buckets and the jumping were perfect ways to develop stability. As the children improved they were given bigger buckets to carry. In addition to building stability, the novices were learning the steps used for attack and defense because the trees were planted in the pattern used for those maneuvers.

Returning to the general program of training, the student who has met the master's initial requirements will move on to the practice of basic sequences. During this time he will practice the sequences until a degree of speed, power, and reaction is achieved. Usually the solutions of the techniques are not taught at this stage. Up to this time the student has been practicing Kung Fu for three years.

The learning and mastery of technique throughout Wu Su training is extremely important. No martial artist can be adequate without the constant practice of techniques. Mastery of technique involves such fundamental considerations as protecting vital areas of the body, speed, power, reaction time, and smoothness. Furthermore, the martial artist should have mastered a large number of techniques. The more techniques a martial artist masters the more effective he will be; possessing a few techniques limits the range of tactics a student has at his disposal while sparring. Because each division usually has at least one hundred barehand techniques, it would be difficult to begin sparring earlier than three years; the three years are needed to build up the proper foundation for fighting. If a person wanted to spar any earlier, he would have to emphasize about twenty techniques and constantly practice them.

After the third year, the student will go on to more complex barehand and weapon sequences. In addition, during this period the solutions of the sequences, techniques of free fighting, human anatomy, herbal treatments, Chinese wrestling, tumbling, throwing darts, horse-riding, bow and arrow, speed and power exercises are learned by the student. The reason most Wu Su students start free fighting only in their third year is due to the fact that the proper reaction time and technique must first be built up to insure that the student will not develop bad habits or get hurt. The sequences usually build up technique while more specific drills will improve reaction against attack. The good martial artist will be the person who has built up his speed and reaction during this training period. If a student starts to spar before speed and reaction time have been trained, he will end up with improper fighting abilities.

During this stage, it is time for the master to pick the formal student. The formal student is a common feature of every style. Usually, a master will pick one or two students and give them special training. The special training will entail almost everything that the master knows. The master picks a formal student because he cannot possibly teach his whole class, which is often composed of about twenty to thirty students, everything he knows while giving each student adequate attention. As a result, the non-formal students learn the common techniques of the style while formal students learn the deeper aspects of the art. By accepting formal training a student must also accept the responsibility of teaching and passing on the name of the style. It is the formal student who will have in-depth knowledge of the particular style. Without the formal student a style could not be passed from generation to generation.

The stage beginning after the student's third year will last about four years; in total the student will spend seven years on external Kung Fu. These seven years will have prepared the student in Wu Su theory and application. At the end of seven years the student is ready for the two most difficult parts of Wu Su: mental training and Chi development.

Mental training involves the development of the martial artist's intuition or feeling, independent of sight, of the presence, intention, or actions of humans, animals, or material things. By having this feeling the martial artist can avoid potentially dangerous situations. For Chinese martial artists it is important to feel whether someone has *Sar Chi* or the "killing mood." If a martial artist can catch this mood he may be able to react before the danger makes itself known. With good intuition the martial artist can sense the slightest movement or presence of people beyond his sight.

The process of gaining this special feeling is divided into two parts. To be able to sense people, or Sar Chi, requires a calm but highly concentrated mind. The calmness and concentration can be obtained by still meditation. Once the martial artist has gained this state of mind, the next stage is to actively train the mind. One way to train is for the martial artist to enter a room full of sandbags in which the only light comes from a candle in a corner, and then punch at the bags. The candle will create many shadows indistinguishable from the sandbags so that it becomes difficult to hit the bags. Only by having a calm and concentrated mind can the martial artist get through this level. The final goal is to use no light while attempting to punch the bags.

The years after external Wu Su are also devoted to the cultivation and use of the powers of Chi. The morality of the student at this point must be of the highest standards if he wishes to achieve the results of Chi training or internal power training. With patience, perseverance and a good master the student can develop many incredible abilities through the proper use of Chi.

One type of Kung Fu which some martial artists (mainly Southern) attempt is the "Golden Bell Cover" (*Gin Chung Tsao*) or "Iron Cloth" (*Tiea Bu Shan*). The Golden Bell Cover is the ability to withstand punches and kicks to the body. The idea is not so much to take a punch (which implies feeling pain but not showing it), but to actually feel no pain when an attack lands. To start this training the master will begin by moderately hitting local areas on the student; by doing this the nerve and muscle system can begin to gradually resist violent agitation. As the nerves and muscles become more resistant, the power of the blows is increased so the tolerance level of the student is also increased. During this type of training many internal bruises may develop which will require the preparation and ingestion of various herbal medicines for their cure.

For the students who have achieved Chi circulation the Golden Bell Cover can be developed to higher levels. During the process of making the nerves and muscles resistant the student practices the ability to direct and concentrate his Chi at the point of attack; the focused Chi makes the student more resistant. In addition, the martial artist can use the Chi to cultivate a rebound force. When an opponent strikes, his attacking power will be directed back like a rubber ball bouncing off a wall. The rebound force is usually so great that the attacker is thrown back.

Training Habits

Up to this point the discussion on Wu Su training has been for the purpose of general information, but now this section will focus on some practical points. Before and during practice, Chinese martial artists will follow a group of common training habits which the student should be aware of:

1. Always concentrate. One of the many possible definitions of Kung Fu is that it is the science of mind over matter. The mind is the true guiding force in Kung Fu; it does not matter if a person is big, small, fast, slow, strong, or weak—what counts is the mind of the martial artist. The key which opens up the mind and its great potential is concentration. Concentration is a relaxed, but extreme, focus of attention. No matter what the martial artist is doing during practice, he should direct his mind and body on the single task he has in front of him. Only by focusing his attention can a martial artist accomplish difficult training procedures. But in concentrating on a task, the student should remain relaxed and calm. By tightening up, the mind gets diverted by tenseness.

   Concentration is so important that a student can accomplish more in one hour of practice, during which he concentrates, than in five hours of practice during which he doesn't concentrate.
2. The best time to start practice is one-half hour before sunrise. This practice should last at least two hours. Later in the day the student should practice one hour after dinner for an additional hour.
3. Before practice do not drink alcohol, smoke, or engage in sex.
4. Do not practice on a completely full or empty stomach.
5. During practice do not eat food or chew gum. Chewing gum can affect breathing during hard exercises.
6. Do not wear jewelry such as watches and rings. Such jewelry can easily cut the skin during practice.
7. If the martial artist is in an extremely bad temper he should not practice. The tightness created by the temper may cause injury to the internal organs.
8. Do not drink water while still puffing from exertion. Rinse out the throat and wait until the breathing returns to normal before drinking. Drinking while puffing may cause injury to the lungs.
9. Do not sit down while puffing.
10. When practicing waist power use a belt. The belt should be tight around the waist (refer to "The Belt in Wu Su").
11. Do not hit the sandbag without knowing the proper techniques. In addition, the student should possess the correct herbal ointments for bruises.
12. Every injury or sore muscle should be treated. These aches and pains may cause arthritis.
13. Immediately put back any dislocated joints. Waiting may cause a bruise inside the joint.
14. When a bone is broken do not massage—see a doctor.
15. If someone is knocked out, massage will help him recover.

The Belt in Wu Su

In some martial systems the practitioners will usually wear colored belts to indicate their rank or status, but in Chinese Wu Su the belt serves a different purpose. In Chinese Wu Su the purpose of the belt is to hold the stomach and intestines in place while a student is practicing. The necessity of holding the stomach and intestines comes about because most Wu Su divisions generate power from the waist.

When power is generated by the waist, the waist must be jerked slightly ahead of a punch. As the jerk occurs, the intestines and stomach receive a violent jolt. Eventually the jolt of the internal organs will cause pain or injury. For this reason an adequately snug belt around the midsection is necessary to hold the stomach and intestines in their normal position. When the belt is worn no pain or injury is caused and the student can continue to practice.

In Chinese Wu Su the belt also differs from the belts used for rank or status in its physical design. The belt in Wu Su is usually six inches wide and about ten feet long. To put the belt on, the student begins by using his belly button as the rough center; once the belt is in place, it is wrapped around the waist so that it is about eight inches wide and must exert firm, but not tight, pressure around the midsection. When the belt reaches the end it is tied in a knot at the side of the waist.

Although the belt in traditional Wu Su has not been used to indicate rank or status, some Kung Fu schools are now imitating other styles and giving colored belts to their students. While the motivations of these schools are good the results are less than desirable. The giving of belts usually makes the student feel that once he achieves the highest possible color rank that there is little more he can learn; the student gets a feeling of false pride in his rank. By abolishing a system of rank the student can learn at his own pace and be motivated by the knowledge he gains—not by the color of his belt.

Chi and Cavities

To properly understand such important things as meditation, striking or pressure points, internal power and massage within the Chinese martial community, the reader must know about Chi and *cavities*. Even outside martial arts the concept of Chi is very important. One of the most central ideas in Chinese medicine is Chi. With the information presented in this section, the reader will have a background in at least understanding some aspects of advanced Kung Fu.

Chi, in many ways, is comparable to blood. Blood, as the operating force of the circulatory system travels an extensive path through the body, nourishing the person and maintaining his general balance of health. Chi, like the blood, also travels through the body. But in the case of Chi, it uses the nerves, a system as extensive as veins and arteries, as its general pathway through the body. Thus, Chi is the operating force of the nervous system. Chi also keeps up the well being and health of the person by providing not a liquid, but a type of electric energy which everybody needs to survive. Chi, in more ways than blood, keeps the human body functioning.

But Chi is different from the blood in one major way. Blood has a constant circulation through the body, while Chi circulates through the nerves following certain patterns. The different Chi cycles that exist in the body will usually follow the cycles of nature. Thus, there are Chi cycles that circulate daily, monthly, seasonally, and yearly. If the circulation is somehow slowed or stopped, then the person will become ill or possibly die. It is therefore vitally important for reasons of health to maintain a smooth circulation of Chi.

For the martial artist Chi takes on significance for various reasons. First, to obtain overall health the martial artist must have a good circulation of Chi through his body. This can be done by two methods: by various systems of meditation or by practicing one of the internal divisions of Kung Fu such as Hsing I or Tai Chi Chuan. Both methods promote Chi circulation by their emphasis on a calm and concentrated mind. Among nonmartial artists, Tai Chi Chuan has become popular because it promotes the flow of Chi, thus making the Tai Chi practitioner improve his health.

Second, Chi is important for the martial artist because it is the basis for internal power. When a martial artist can properly tap, concentrate, and use the Chi of his body, he can have power that goes beyond the strength of the muscles. (The power generated by the muscles is called external power.) With internal power the martial artist can do many incredible feats of strength that go beyond the mere use of the muscles. A martial artist becomes truly advanced when he can use internal power for martial purposes.

Although the achievement of internal power is one of the ultimate goals in Chinese Wu Su, few martial artists have developed it. To develop internal power requires that the martial artist have a smooth circulation of Chi; this by itself requires time. After obtaining a smooth flow of Chi, the martial artist must train with a competent master in extremely difficult exercises which develop his capacity to use Chi. To obtain a smooth circulation of Chi, to find a good master, and to practice the rigorous training methods will take at least ten years of devoted practice. Very few martial artists have been able to go the distance.

The third important aspect of Chi for the martial artist is its relationship to acupuncture. As noted earlier, Chi circulates through the nerves; but because it travels through the nerves it may be affected at special points where the nerves become exposed or are sensitive to stimulation. By stimulating those special points, the circulation of Chi can be affected. It is those points which acupuncturists needle to produce good health. These points are also called cavities.

Cavities or acupuncture points become very important for the martial artist. To understand why they are important it is necessary to understand the acupuncture "meridian." The nerve system on which a cavity is located will have connections which travel to certain internal organs. The specific nerve path and its route in the body is the meridian. The body as a whole contains 12 meridians and 2 vessels through which Chi circulates. Therefore, if a meridian through its cavity is agitated or stimulated, the internal organ controlled by the meridian will also receive the stimulation; a gentle stimulus will thus prod the internal organs into better functioning—this is what the acupuncture needle does. But if the cavity receives a violent strike, the meridian and the internal organs controlled by it will be disrupted and damaged. As an example, nearly everybody has felt the pain caused by hitting the funny bone, a cavity. In addition to pain, there is also temporary paralysis of the arm. Extending this to a more important cavity such as one located in the armpit, the Ghi Chuan cavity, which lies on a meridian passing through the heart, it is easy to see how a powerful strike to this cavity can cause a shock wave to pass into the heart the same way a strike to the funny bone causes a shock wave to pass into the arm. A powerful blow to the cavity located in the armpit can cause a person to die of heart failure.

For these reasons, Chinese martial artists have found 108 cavities (out of a possible 700 cavities used by acupuncturists) which can be used for martial purposes. Many divisions will keep the locations of the cavities secret, but in all they are the same 108 cavities. Of the 108 cavities, 72 are used to cause fainting or local paralysis, and 36 are used to cause death.

Cavities are also important in helping to cure certain injuries. When a bruise from an attack occurs it may get lodged in a cavity. Once in the cavity, the bruise can affect Chi circulation and thus the person's health. Massage and herbal treatments are then used to force the bruise out of the cavity. If a serious bruise occurs in a cavity vital for the circulation of Chi, then the person may die if the bruise is not removed. Although a bruise may become lodged in a cavity, sometimes the ill effects are not seen for a certain time period because the Chi has not yet reached the damaged cavity; such effects depend on the nature of the cavity. For the serious cases massage and special herbs are used as cures.

It can be readily seen that a knowledge of Chi and its relationship to acupuncture is important for a martial artist. For fighting or for health, Chi and its various aspects are important. It is obvious from this discussion that a good martial artist must know more than mere punching and kicking.

Iron Sand Hand (or Palm)

The seemingly incredible feats of breaking hard objects such as wood planks and bricks are much admired by Western audiences. However, the audiences and even the performers are many times ignorant of the principles behind such actions. In fact, many martial artists who break hard objects end up giving themselves long term injuries which show up later in life. This fact is all the more important because many instructors push students into the practice of breaking hard objects without knowing the purpose or general theory. This section, then, will hopefully give the student an adequate understanding of the general subject in order that he may avoid causing himself unnecessary injury.

In China the ability to break hard objects has been known for hundreds of years. This ability has been generally known as the *Iron Sand* or *Red Sand Hand* (or *Palm*). Many Chinese Wu Su divisions have their own methods of developing the Iron Sand Hand. While the methods may differ the principles behind each system are the same.

The most important fact in guiding the development of the Iron Sand Hand is a simple physiological fact: any time a person forcefully hits a hard object with his hand, the nerves will be damaged and a bruise will form on the bones or inside the joints. It is easy to see that breaking hard objects may cause unnecessary and permanent damage if the hand is not properly treated.

Through years of research Chinese martial artists have developed methods which give them great power in their hands but which do not cause permanent injury to the nerves, bones, or muscles. The basic principle behind every method is to progressively condition the bones, nerves, and muscles to greater levels of shock while using herbs to cure any injury to the hand. At each stage (there are usually ten to twelve stages depending on the style—in White Crane there are twelve stages) a different herb must be used to accommodate the growing severity of the training methods. Only by using herbs at each stage can the hand move on to more resistance. The whole process takes at least *three* years; if the process is shortened, the hand will not have enough time to heal itself with the help of the herbs. Injury to the hand as a result of speeding up the training process may be seen in some martial artists of non-Kung Fu styles. Many of these martial artists progress much too quickly (many do not even use herbs) to the breaking of bricks or planks. Sometimes the whole time period will be less than three months. It can be observed that these martial artists cannot extend and hold their hands steady. The hands will tremble uncontrollably, because the nerves, muscles, and Chi circulation have been affected by the internal bruises. In terms of long range damage, the overly quick jump to breaking bricks and planks will cause arthritis in later life.

The Iron Sand Hand gets its name from the last stage of training which is the most dangerous. At this stage an oval kettle is filled with iron filings or sand and heated up (the name Red Sand Hand comes from the color of the sand as it is heated). The martial artist then plunges his hand into the kettle and stirs the sand using prescribed methods. The nerves of the hand at this stage are given a tremendous amount of stress by the hot iron filings or sand. For this reason, the herb used at this final stage is extremely poisonous and must be applied with caution.

The ultimate test of the Iron Sand Hand is to place twelve bricks on a flat floor with nothing between them (some martial styles slightly separate every brick from each other and the floor by small pieces of wood) and break every brick by the slap of the palm. The truly great martial artists who possess the Iron Sand Hand have such control that they can break any brick at any level. Such martial artists can easily direct their power to any depth of an opponent's body.

As a warning to the potential student, he should realize that the training of the Iron Sand Hand requires a qualified master. To attempt this without a master will only result in the student injuring himself. In addition, he should also realize that many of the necessary herbs are to be found only in Asia and can only be bought at a great price.

Although the Iron Sand Hand is a great possession it has one great drawback. The martial artist who goes beyond eight to ten stages will become sterile. According to acupuncture theory, the nerves in the hand can influence the reproductive organs (the testicles) if enough stimulus is given to the hands. It is clear that the training methods can easily do this. Usually, martial artists who already have children or are permanent bachelors will go beyond the eighth or tenth stage.

CHAPTER 2
FUNDAMENTAL
TRAINING AND
PRACTICE

This chapter is the most important in the book for the beginning student. In this chapter the beginning student will be shown in detail various aspects which range from fundamental to advanced; such sections as those on hand and leg techniques will contain both simple and difficult punches and kicks. The wide range of subsections (warm-up, stretching, moving techniques, hand techniques, leg techniques, power and speed training, and striking zones) is intended to give the student a wide exposure to many important aspects of basic training. Many of the forms and techniques can be learned almost completely from the photographs and explanations, while others may require some help from a qualified master. In addition to detailing techniques, every subsection will have an introductory segment discussing the general theory behind the subject.

WARM UP AND STRETCHING

Warm Up

Before the student begins any practice session he should first warm up. By warming up the student can prevent needless injuries because he will have toned his body to anticipate fast and violent motion. Secondly, by warming up the martial artist can practice much longer. While the student is warming up he should observe a few general rules: first, stay relaxed; second, each warm up exercise should be done 30 to 40 times or for one or two minutes; third, warm up before practice; fourth, if the weather is cool, warm up longer than usual.

Figure 1: Rotate the head in a circular motion, changing directions every 15 seconds. This exercise loosens the neck.

Figure 2: Keep your arms at your side and moderately shake your whole arm from shoulder to fingers. To help this motion, bounce at the knees. This exercise loosens the fingers, wrist, elbow, and shoulder.

Figure 3: Keeping the feet parallel, swing the arms—one up and one down—and the waist from side to side as far as possible. The head should point forwards at all times. This loosens the neck, shoulder, arms, and stomach.

1   2   3

Figures 4, 5: Swing the arms down and up forming a circle while keeping the knees firm. When the arms reach the top of the circle, bend the back. This loosens the back and stomach.

Figure 6: Stand with feet parallel and rotate in a circle moving only the hips. Bend as far forward and backward as possible while keeping the knees locked. This loosens the hips and back.

4

5

6

Figure 7: Stand with feet together and hands on knees while rotating the knees in a circle down and forward. Keep the feet flat at all times. This loosens the knees and hips.

Figure 8: Pivot the toe of one foot firmly on the ground and rotate the ankle by forming a circle. Reverse rotation every 15 seconds.

Figure 9: Stand with feet parallel and with knees locked while bending and touching your toes. The legs can be spread further apart for stretching the inside thigh muscle. This loosens the legs and back.

Figure 10: Stand with the legs apart and feet parallel. Swing one arm in a forward motion down and up while turning the waist in the same direction. At the same time swing the other arm back, down and up. The body at this point is a triangle. Reverse directions by bringing the arms down again and up while turning the waist. At every third swing the arms should make a complete circle over the head. This warm up exercise is necessary after vigorous punching because the muscles usually become very tight. It loosens the shoulder, back, and chest.

7

8

9

10

Stretching

After the warm up, it is necessary for certain heavily used muscles to be stretched. These muscles must be stretched because over-elongation will cause them to violently contract and thus cause injury. By proper stretching, the muscle can go farther in its elongation; the greater the muscle can extend or elongate itself the less chance for injury. A few general rules for stretching should be followed. First, always warm up before stretching. Second, spend at least five minutes in stretching a major muscle. One of the most important of the major muscles that must be stretched is the thigh. (Other major muscles are the calf, stomach, shoulder, and back.) The thigh has four separate muscle systems which must all be properly stretched: those muscles are located on the front, back, side, and inside. In this volume the student can pick his own stretching exercise for each system because a number of different exercises are shown. Third, stretching should always be easy. Use only gentle force while pushing the muscle. Some students must be patient because they may not become properly stretched for awhile.

Figure 11: Bring the feet together while bending forward. Touch your palms to the ground or your forehead to your knees. This stretches the back and back of the thighs.

Figure 12: Keeping the knees locked, turn your waist and touch your palms to the side of your feet. This stretches the side of the thighs, side of the waist, and shoulder.

Figure 13: Extend one leg and keep its knee stiff while touching your toes. Touch your forehead to your knee if possible. This stretches the back, shoulder, and back of the thighs.

13

11

12

Figure 14: Place your ankle so that the bottom of the foot is at a 90 degree angle to the ground. Bend forward to touch your foot with your forehead. This stretches the side of the thighs and ankles.

Figure 15: Spread legs as far as possible and touch hands to toes or forehead to leg. This stretches the back, back of the thighs, inside of the thighs, and shoulder.

Figure 16: Same as previous exercise except legs are together. This stretches the back, shoulder, and back of the thighs.

Figure 17: Keep one leg locked and touch your hands to your toe. This stretches the ankle and inside of the thighs.

Figure 18: Place your ankle flat and touch your hand to your foot. This stretches the ankle, inside of the thighs, back, and shoulder.

Figure 19: The leg being stretched should remain straight. If possible, touch your forehead to your leg. This stretches the back, shoulder, and back of the thighs.

Figure 20: Place bottom of feet together and bend forward. This stretches the back, inside of the thighs, and side of the thighs.

Figure 21: Spread legs as far as possible and lower your head to the floor. This stretches the back, inside of the thighs, and back of the thighs.

Figure 22: Split legs with feet parallel and swing your upper body forward and backward. This stretches the back, inside of the thighs, and waist.

Figure 23: This type of split differs from others by having the back ankle resting on the ground. This split should be done gradually until the legs can be fully extended. This stretches the inside of the thighs and back of the thighs.

Figure 24: Bend one leg flat in front of your abdomen and touch the ground in front of your knee with your forehead. Keep the other leg straight and its foot level. This stretches the side of the thighs, inside of the thighs, and ankle.

Figure 25: Sit on your knees and then bend backwards and touch your head to the ground. This stretches the front of the thighs, stomach, and chest.

14

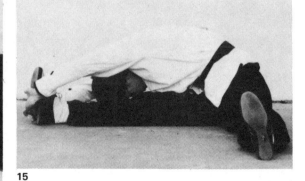

15

16   17

18

19

20

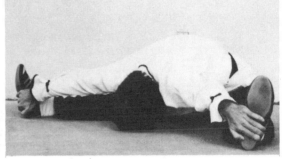

21

22

23

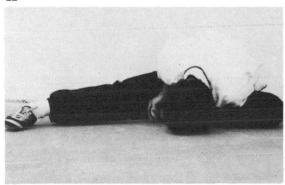

24

25

Figure 26: Start with your back on the ground and then raise your body up on the hands and legs. Fingers are pointing toward your toes. This stretches the front of the thighs, back, stomach, and arms.

Figure 27: Place instep of foot on a raised ledge and bend backward. This stretches the front of the thighs and stomach.

Figure 28: Grab the instep of one leg and pull back as far as possible. This stretches the front of the thighs and stomach.

Figure 29: Raise your leg up and touch your toe to your forehead. This stretches the side of the thighs.

26

27

28

29

FUNDAMENTAL STANCES

Stances are extremely important in Chinese Wu Su because they are the foundation of all movement. The starting and ending point of every defensive or offensive technique is a particular stance. In many cases shifting to a certain stance will be the key point in moving away from or into an opponent. Because stances are so important, a wide variety have been devised to fit many situations. Some stances may distribute the body's weight equally on both legs, while other stances may put all the weight on one leg. Some styles even have their own particular stances or emphasize one stance more than others. Although the stances vary in their form and purpose, they are all guided by a few basic principles.

The first and most important principle guiding the use of a stance is stability. Dynamically, stability is achieved by a low center of gravity; the lower something is to the ground, the harder it is to knock down. In any stance, then, the lower the student stands, the lower his center of gravity becomes. Stability is thus increased by a low stance. Although low stances are extremely important in Wu Su, there does exist a group of high stances which are meant only for very quick defense, attack, or withdrawal techniques.

To obtain a low stance the martial artist must observe two points. First, with any low stance the knees must be bent and flexible. By bending the knees the center of gravity is lowered to create a more stable foundation. The bending of the knees must be flexible in order to move quickly and smoothly. Second, the back is usually kept straight. By keeping the back straight the weight of the body does not lean too far forward or backward; the torso's weight is then on the same line as the center of gravity.

By having a low stance the martial artist gains another advantage besides stability; he gains smoother and quicker movements. At first glance it would seem that a low stance might interfere with some types of movement. But this is not the case if a martial artist constantly practices low stances and low movements. The student will find that once he is comfortable, the speed and agility of techniques are greatly improved. Only by constant practice can low stances be made effective.

A second major trait to consider in a stance is its capacity to protect vital areas of the body. Stances which expose too much body area are bound to fail. Usually the main reason for improper protection of vital areas is the high stance. By standing high a person exposes more body area, and thus more area for an opponent's attack. As mentioned before, Chinese Wu Su does have a few high stances, but the stances are constructed in such a manner that they seal the vital areas of the body. In contrast, low stances provide adequate protection of vital areas.

As mentioned before, stances are of extreme importance in movement. Of the ten stances explained in this chapter a few stances, such as Dsao Pan Bu, are used for continuous movement. Such stances would be used in free fighting to move into or away from an opponent. Other stances such as Gin Gi Du Li are used only as transitions between techniques. Either way, both types of stances are necessary for the complete martial artist.

1. *Ma Bu* (fig. 30)

    Ma Bu (the "horse" stance) is the most fundamental of all Wu Su stances. The Ma Bu that will be taught in this book is different from the horse stances of some styles. To assume this stance, place the feet parallel slightly beyond shoulder width. Move the knees down and inward until a 90 degree angle is formed between the back part of the calf and the thigh. The back should be straight. Ma Bu is especially valuable in building up the strength of the knees. The beginning student should try

30   31   32

to stand in Ma Bu for at least five minutes but no longer than ten. During Ma Bu training it is important to concentrate on directing the power of the legs straight down and not to the side. To practice this stance the student should begin by standing straight with both feet together and the hands at the waist in a fist. With a slight jump switch into Ma Bu at the same time punching out with both hands. With another slight jump return to the original position and repeat the drill.

2. **Deng San Bu** (figs. 31, 32)

Deng San Bu (the "mountain climbing" stance) is one of the most commonly used offensive stances; kicks and punches are easily delivered from its position. In this stance roughly 60 percent of the weight is on the front leg and 40 percent on the back. The front knee is over the ankle and the back leg should be stiff. The front foot should be turned in about 15 degrees and the hips should face the direction of the forward leg.

To practice this stance (together with Ma Bu) begin by starting in Ma Bu with the fists at the waist (palms pointing up). Move the left hand across the body in a counterclockwise motion to block an imagined punch. The palms at this point should point out (fig. 31).Move the left hand back to the waist while at the same time punching out with the right hand and shifting into Deng San Bu. The left foot will have 60 percent of the weight and the face should point to the front (fig. 32). With the extended right hand, make a circle going clockwise with palms facing out; this motion is another block. Pull the right hand in and punch out with the left while shifting 180 degrees into a Deng San Bu that has the right leg receiving 60 percent of the weight. While shifting into Deng San Bu, the student uses Ma Bu as a transition stance. Keep repeating.

3. **Dsao Pan Bu** (figs. 33, 34)

Dsao Pan Bu (the "sitting with crossed legs" stance) is a very important stance because it is the foundation of *crab walking* (see "Theory and Techniques of Movement"). This stance can be used for either attack or defense. To assume this stance first stand in Ma Bu. Next, raise the left toe while pivoting on the left heel. At the same time, turn left until the body is facing in the opposite direction. During the turn the right foot pivots and turns on its toe (fig. 33). Bend the knees until the right heel is about one inch off the ground (fig. 34). In this final position the left foot is flat and the right is on its toes.

34

33   34   35

To practice this stance, as the student is turning his back he should swing his left arm around to block an imagined punch (see fig. 33). Before the feet are planted punch out with the right hand. Return to the original position. The stance and its practice can also be done by turning to the right side; in this case the directions are mirror images.

4. *Ssu Lieu Bu* (fig. 35)

Ssu Lieu Bu (the "four six" stance) is one of the most versatile stances in Wu Su. From this stance the martial artist can switch into various techniques with relative ease. In this stance 40 percent of the weight is on the front leg, while 60 percent is on the back leg. The knee of the front leg should be turned slightly inward and bent. Never make the front knee straight in this stance; if a kick were to land on the stiffened knee, it could easily break it. The front foot should be at a 30 degree angle. In addition, the back knee must be flexed and turned inward toward the groin.

To change into Ssu Lieu Bu from Ma Bu, turn the body to either direction so that the back leg has 60 percent of the total weight and the front has 40 percent of the weight. As the student shifts he should position his hands so that the lead hand is pushing out, while the back hand is in front of the chest. In Ssu Lieu Bu the lead hand is always the one on the same side as the front leg. Shifting from Ma Bu will help develop speed and stability.

Another good way to practice Ssu Lieu Bu is to change direction 180 degrees using this stance. Starting from a Ssu Lieu Bu which faces the right side as in figure 35, begin turning the body conterclockwise while at the same time putting the back of the left hand under the right triceps. As the body is making the turn, slide the left hand along the right arm going toward the fist area. At the point where the body is 90 degrees from the original position, the student should be in Ma Bu with the left hand still under the right arm. Keep turning counterclockwise until 60 percent of the weight is on the back (right) leg—at this instant, the left hand finishes its slide up the right arm and is then thrust out with palms facing front. The right hand then moves slightly in front of the chest. Repeat by going back to the original position using the same method but opposite hands.

5. *Fu Hu Bu* (fig. 36)

Fu Hu Bu (the "tame the tiger" stance) is generally used as a defense against high attacks such as jump kicks. This stance has a particularly interesting origin

36   37   38

which reflects its use against high attacks. During the Sung dynasty (about 420 A.D.) a famous hero named Wu Shong was in the jungle when he was suddenly attacked by a huge tiger. As the tiger leapt at him, Wu Shong withdrew his only weapon, a small dagger, and bent low to avoid the leaping tiger. When the tiger was above him, Wu Shong stabbed the tiger in the belly and killed him. Wu Shong thus tamed the tiger.

To assume this stance begin by standing in Ma Bu. Squat down on the left leg until your thigh is parallel to the ground. The right leg should be extended straight out to the side. Both feet must be planted flat and the back is straight (fig. 36). To practice this stance first assume figure 36. Shift the weight onto the right leg while raising the right hand and swinging the left hand across the body: the hand motion is a block up and a strike down. Once the weight has shifted to the right leg, the left leg is held straight. Repeat.

6. *Gin Gi Du Li* (fig. 37)

Gin Gi Du Li (the "golden rooster stands by one leg" stance) is generally used for quick leg attacks. To assume this stance raise one leg until the knee is as high as possible. The hand on the same side of the raised knee should be extended with the palm facing out: this protects the chest. The opposite hand is near the head with the palm facing to the side (fig. 37). This stance is especially useful in training overall stability and kicking speed. To do this the student assumes the stance and kicks with the raised leg as quickly as possible. The kicking leg should not be set down at any moment during the series of rapid kicks.

To practice the stance itself, assume the position of figure 37. Step down with the right leg and begin turning in a 180 degree counterclockwise direction while raising the left leg. At the same time bring both arms in front of the chest and cross them in an "x" shape. At the moment that the body is completely turned and the left leg raised, thrust out with the left hand. The right arm should be near the head with palm out and elbow pointing back. Repeat the process going back to the original position.

7. *Sheun Gi Bu* (fig. 38)

Sheun Gi Bu (the "false" stance) like Gin Gi Du Li can be used for quick kicking. To assume this stance, place all the body's weight on one leg and lightly touch the ground with the opposite leg. The arm opposite the lead leg is extended in front of the face. The other hand is extended back and down with the fingertips touching each other.

39

40

41

The movements for this stance are almost the same as Gin Gi Du Li. Turn the body conterclockwise 180 degrees, shifting the weight from the back foot to the front foot while bringing the hands to the chest in an "x" shape. When the weight has shifted and the turn is complete, make sure the lead leg has no weight on it and the arms are out in their correct position; the hand opposite the lead leg should be forward and the other in back.

8. **Tun Bu** (fig. 39)

Tun Bu (the "swallow" stance) is similar to Fu Hu Bu in being a low defensive form. To assume this stance squat on one leg putting about 90 percent of the weight on it. The thigh of the bent leg should be parallel to the ground with the back straight. The opposite leg is extended straight and on its heel. The arms are the same as in Gin Gi Du Li.

The practice of this stance is also similar to Fu Hu Bu. Once in the stance move the weight of the body onto the straight leg while turning the torso 180 degrees clockwise. As the weight shifts on the lead foot turn the toe of the right leg up. The movements of the hands are exactly as in Gin Gi Du Li. To return to the original position turn counterclockwise. Keep repeating.

9. **Chi Lin Bu** (fig. 40)

Chi Lin Bu (the "unicorn" stance) is another extremely versatile stance; the martial artist can easily move backward while having the ability to kick from the rear leg. The name of this form, the unicorn stance, comes from the belief that a unicorn had to bend its knee in order to bow. To assume this stance start in Ma Bu. Next, place the right leg behind the left leg while turning the upper body to the right side. The knee of the right leg should be one inch above the ground and behind the left ankle. The right leg is on its toes and 90 degrees to the left foot. The left leg has about 80 percent of the weight. Place the arms as in figure 40. To assume this stance in the opposite direction, merely switch right for left and left for right. This stance is commonly used for withdrawal. To practice withdrawal using this stance, refer to "Theory and Techniques of Movement" in this chapter.

10. **Dsao Dun** (fig. 41)

Dsao Dun (the "squat" stance) is used mainly to build up the thigh and knee muscles. To assume Dsao Dun stand in Ma Bu and squat down until the thighs are parallel to the ground. The back must remain straight and the hands should slightly cup the knees. The student should not attempt to stand in Dsao Dun if he has not built up the strength of the knees. Standing in Dsao Dun with weak knees can cause damage to the ligaments.

THEORY AND TECHNIQUES OF MOVEMENT

Theory

The first emphasis in Chinese Wu Su is on defense. Attack is only taught once the student has mastered the techniques of blocking, dodging, escaping, and withdrawal. This priority contrasts with other Eastern martial styles which mainly stress attack. In Wu Su it is believed that if a student has gained proficiency in defense, then attack will come with little effort because defense requires a good knowledge of attack strategies. The student who knows defense has automatically laid a foundation for attack. In the end, the student who learns defense first, and attack afterwards, will have an advantage over the student who learns attack first.

Overall, the basic purpose of dodging, escaping, and withdrawal techniques is to avoid being hit while creating an advantageous situation for the defender—whatever the advantage may be. Immediately implied in this definition is the avoidance of slugging it out or taking the pill. It is useless to stand in one spot and continuously punch or kick an opponent who is also doing the same thing. This way of thinking leads the martial arts to become a system where only those who can slug it out will win; this negates the whole spirit of Kung Fu and is totally *impractical*.

Behind each method of dodging, escaping, and withdrawal lies important guiding principles. The first consideration is stability. It is very easy to get knocked down while moving if stability is lacking. Stability means, as it does in stances, a low form. As the student practices each technique he should be conscious of staying low and directing his leg power down, almost as if he were glued to the ground.

The second consideration is the protection of vital parts of the body or cavities (from this point the word cavities refers to the vital areas of the body: see "Attack Zones"). Moving forms are useless if an opponent can strike an important cavity. A large part of a martial artist's success depends on positioning himself so that only strong areas with few cavities are exposed. Having low forms helps the protection of cavities tremendously. Additionally, each moving form must allow the martial artist to protect or seal exposed cavities through blocks, body movement, or an extended hand which covers the body.

The third important aspect of a moving form is speed. Speed is a matter of being quick while moving in a prescribed manner. As the student practices he should try to make each moving form come alive. By concentrating on speed during practice, the student can apply offensive and defensive techniques with ease. Quickness only comes about by continual practice.

While stability, protection of cavities, and speed deal with the specific components of moving forms there is, in addition, the strategic ideas of movement. The first strategic concept is the idea of distance. In Chinese martial theory the distance a martial artist stands from his opponent can be classified into three categories: short, middle, and long range. Each category has its own special consideration and problems.

The first category of short range is defined as the area in which two martial artists can kick or punch each other without having to move. The short range occurs when people are standing face-to-face and can touch each other by any amount of arm or leg extension. The short range is a danger zone in the sense that the student can be hit at any instant. In the short range the student must mainly be proficient in hand techniques since many kicks are difficult to execute at this range.

The middle range is the distance between two people such that a short hop, jump, skip, or step must be taken to move into the short range (striking distance). In the middle range, a martial artist is slightly out of reach of a punch or kick; he must move a small step if he wishes to attack. Although kicks are easier to execute in this range, hands and legs are of equal importance for middle range sparring.

Long range, the last category, requires that a martial artist take two or more steps to be in the short range. This contrasts with the middle range in that a large jump or series of steps is required to reach the opponent. The long range is relatively safe because most attacks can be avoided due to the distance that must be crossed. Still, the good martial artist should never be overconfident about feeling safe in any range.

In Chinese Wu Su many styles can be identified by the range they typically occupy. Styles like Long Fist and Northern Praying Mantis are highly specialized for long and middle range, while styles like White Crane and Tiger are specialized for middle and short range. No matter what style the student is studying, he should be constantly aware of the distance between him and his opponent. Also, the martial artist should have the capacity to move into any range with ease, stability, and quickness.

A vital issue which deals with the concept of distance is the size of the field used for free fighting or sparring competition. Because almost every Wu Su style teaches dodging, escaping, and withdrawal, the size of the field for competition becomes extremely important. To restrict the field to an overly small area would be unfair and impractical. It would be unfair in the sense that a style which specializes in middle or short range fighting such as White Crane would automatically have an advantage over a style such as Long Fist, which specializes in long and middle range techniques. The main ideal of competition is to allow both sides to start on an equal footing.

An overly small area is also impractical in the sense that a majority of real fights do not take place in a small boundary which is arbitrarily set. A martial artist who is attacked on a street or inside most buildings will usually have some room to maneuver. This issue can be seen with more clarity at some martial tournaments. At most tournaments the area is usually restricted to about 10 to 15 square feet; this type of area allows little room for many defensive maneuvers. In such an area a person can bully his way to victory with wild uncoordinated punches and kicks; the attack may never land but it has forced the other person out of the ring, which results in an automatic loss. The person who bullies his way has no need to fear retaliation since much of his body is off-limits to punches and kicks.

A fair field of competition, then, would be the area of a boxing ring. In that type of area a martial artist must show his skills in terms of realistic fighting because such a field would require all-around abilities of attack and defense. Some may raise the objection that a long range specialist like a Long Fist practitioner will then have an advantage in such a field; but such an objection does not really hold, because the ability to maneuver and corner an opponent is a vital skill in real fighting.

Another aspect related to the concept of distance is the idea of a "door" (*Men*). As a martial artist approaches an opponent he has three options; he may approach an opponent from the opponent's right side, left side, or front. Each one of these options or directions is called a door. Thus if a martial artist approaches from the opponent's left side, the martial artist is attempting to enter the left door. In Chinese Wu Su there are some techniques which are specifically constructed for certain doors.

As the martial artist attempts to enter one of the doors he may find the door "open" (*Kun Men*) or "closed" (*Bi Men*). If the door is open, then the cavities are exposed and easily attacked. If the door is closed, the cavities are protected in some way and are not accessible to attack. Although a door may be closed, it is still possible for a martial artist to use certain techniques to force it open. A common way to force a door to open is to fake a kick or punch in order to make an opponent react by committing himself to a certain action which will open one of his doors. When the opponent commits himself because of the fake, the martial artist can attack through the open door.

It is usually impossible to keep all three doors closed simultaneously. For this reason a good martial artist will show only a closed door to the opponent while sparring. Even though it is important to guard against attacks directed to an open door, it is also important to have the capacity to attack through an open door. Both abilities are vital for the competent martial artist.

Turning now to the nine forms explained in this volume, the student should be aware of some distinctions in their particular use. In essence, it is necessary to differentiate the terms dodge, withdrawal, escape, and forcing. A dodge is a short quick movement backward or to the side. A withdrawal is a movement going one or two steps backward. An escape is a continuous withdrawal. And last, forcing is a continuous intense movement into an opponent which forces him to move in a certain direction. Forcing is generally used to set up an opponent for an attack.

Techniques of Movement

42   43

1. *Hsing Bu* (fig. 42)

   This form is performed like everyday walking but with some important exceptions. In *Hsing Bu* ("walking steps") the knees are bent and close together, thus protecting the groin. When walking the body should be low and the back straight with the weight placed on the outer edges of the foot. If the student walks on his heels the head will start bobbing up and down and a headache will eventually occur. When walking Hsing Bu, one hand should be held forward protecting the chest while the other hand should be in the back with all its finger-tips touching each other. If the student wants to reverse direction he should turn to the side opposite of his lead foot and cross the front and rear hand. Crossing of the hands protects the chest while the student is reversing directions. In reversing direction, the back leg and arm become the forward extensions. To practice this form the student should walk back and forth or in a circle while periodically changing directions. Hsien Bu is extremely useful in escape, dodge, or attack.

2. *Chai Twe* (fig. 43)

   Chai Twe ("Step-on-steps") is a constant blocking and kicking move. This form can be used to chase an opponent. To start this form begin with feet together. With the left hand block up with palm facing out while kicking Teng Twe (see "Kicking Techniques") using the right leg. The key point in this form is to keep low; keeping low will develop knee power. In real fighting this kick can go to the opponent's knee or belly. Once the right leg kicks out, step down with it, block with the right hand, and kick Teng Twe with the left foot. Keep repeating while moving forward.

3. *Yiou Bu* (figs. 44, 45)

   Yiou Bu ("hop jump") is used extensively in the middle range: it can be used for quick entry into the short range for attack, or quick retreat into long range to avoid

44

46

48

45

47

49

attack. To begin assume Ssu Lieu Bu (fig. 44). To move forward push off the rear leg so that a short hop is executed and land in the original stance. While hopping both legs should be spread apart as in figure 45. Do not bring the rear leg too close to the front leg. Keep repeating. To move backward, push off the front leg and once again land in the original stance.

4. **Tiao Bu** (figs. 46, 47)

Tiao Bu ("jump steps") is a moving form that can be used for escape and attack. In this form the student can move forward or backward by simply jumping off one leg while raising the other as high as possible. While jumping the knee must be raised high to protect the groin. This motion is actually a skipping action that raises the knees as high as possible.

5. **Shei Bu** (figs. 48, 49)

Shei Bu ("crab walking") is also popularly called Tou Bu which means "clandestine steps." This extremely effective form gets its name from the walking motion of a crab. Crab walking can be used for escaping, dodging, forcing, or for entering the short range. While moving in this form major cavities are well protected. In addition, it allows quick attack with the rear leg or lead arm. To start this form begin by assuming Dsao Pan Bu (see "Fundamental Stances"). Once the legs are crossed, the student can move in a forward or backward direction by continually crossing the legs. While moving, the body should be low and the arms out to protect the chest.

50   51   52

6. *Huo Tiao* (figs. 50, 51, 52)

Huo Tiao, (the "white crane jump") is used for dodging and escaping. Begin by assuming the stance in figure 50: the hands are in a blocking position and the right leg is ready to kick. Next, kick Ti Twe (see "Leg Techniques") as high as possible (fig. 51). Remember, kick high in practice to develop speed and power, but in real fighting kick low. After kicking, set the right leg down and jump off it going backwards. Land in the original position (fig. 50). Keep repeating. Later switch kicking feet.

53   54   55

7. *Chi Lin Tiao* (figs. 53, 54, 55)

Chi Lin Tiao ("unicorn jumping") can be used for escaping while retaining the ability to kick. To start, begin by assuming the unicorn stance or Chi Lin Bu (fig. 53). Bring the rear leg up and kick Teng Twe (fig. 54). Bring the kicking leg to its original position and jump off it going backwards. While in the air the left forward leg crosses the right (fig. 55) so that the student will first touch down on his left leg. Once the left leg touches down, the right leg is immediately brought behind it to assume the original position. Kick again with the right leg and begin the backward jump. Later switch legs so that the left leg kicks. The directions are the same except for the switching of right and left.

56   57   58

8.   *Tzon Tiao* (figs. 56, 57, 58)

    Tzon Tiao ("side jump") is another White Crane method used mainly for escape. Start by assuming the stance in figure 56. The left hand is in the shape of a White Crane Wing (see "Hand Forms") and is used to protect the upper body. Kick 45 degrees to the right side with the right leg using Chei Twe (fig. 57). Figure 57 is the kick viewed from the front. Put the right leg down and jump off it to the right side while crossing the hands as in figure 58. When the student lands he is in a mirror position of figure 57: his right hand is forward in the White Crane Wing and his left leg is extended. The student then kicks Chei Twe 45 degrees to his left side with his left leg. He then sets his left leg down and jumps off it going to the left side while crossing his hands. Once he lands he is in the original starting position (fig. 56). Repeat this process. The student will be making a zig-zag pattern as he moves forward or backward.

59   60   61

9.   *Dan Tiao* (figs. 59, 60, 61)

    Dan Tiao ("single leg hop") is mainly used to get into the middle or short range during sparring. To begin, assume Ssu Lieu Bu with left leg forward and the left arm extended (fig. 59). With the left hand make a block by moving it counterclockwise with the palms facing out while raising the left knee (fig. 60). Then with the left leg step forward and skip (fig. 61). Land in Ssu Lieu Bu with the right leg forward. As the student comes down he should punch out with his right hand. He then blocks with his right arm moving clockwise while raising the right knee. Step forward with the right leg and skip. Punch while landing so that the original position is once again assumed (fig. 59). Keep repeating.

HAND TECHNIQUES

Hand Forms

There are more than twenty hand forms used for blocking and attacking in Chinese Wu Su. In this section, hand forms which are most popular with Wu Su practitioners will be shown. Because the pictures of the hand forms are self-explanatory, no detailed descriptions will be given. In order for the student to get an idea of the practicality of the hand forms, this section will include a discussion on the application of a few forms.

Table 1 Hand Forms

Figure	Name	Main Division(s)
62	*Chuan* ("Fist")	All Divisions
63	*Chuai Sou* ("Hammer Hand")	White Crane
64	*Gung Sou* ("Double Finger Fist")	White Crane
65	*Dan Tzu Gieh* ("Single Finger Fist")	White Crane
66	*Kua Chuan* ("Detour Hook Fist")	Long Fist, Praying Mantis
67	*Dan Sou* ("Finger Tip Hand")	White Crane, Long Fist, Eagle
68	*Ien Jsui* ("Eagle Beak")	Eagle, Tai Chi, Long Fist, Praying Mantis
69	*Huo Jsui* ("White Crane Beak")	White Crane
70	*Tan Lan Sou* ("Praying Mantis Hand")	Praying Mantis
71	*Ien Chao* ("Eagle Claw")	Eagle
72	*Huo Chao* ("White Crane Claw")	White Crane
73	*Don Chao* ("Dragon Claw")	Dragon
74	*Bao Chao* ("Panther Claw")	Panther
75	*Fu Chao* ("Tiger Claw")	Tiger
76, 77	*Huo Chiz* ("White Crane Wing")	White Crane
78	*Chang* ("Palm") Zone A	All Divisions
	Sou Dau ("Hand Knife") Zone B	All Divisions
	Chiz ("Sting") Zone C	All Divisions

79	*Chien Chueh*	All Divisions
	("Sword Secret")	
	Used for the symmetric flow of the internal energy with the narrow blade sword.	
80	*Chien Bie*	All Divisions
	("Forearm")	
81	*Zou*	All Divisions
	("Elbow")	
82	*Gen*	All Divisions
	("Shoulder")	

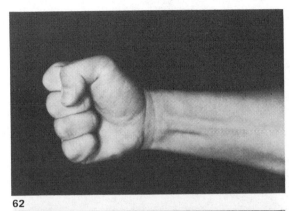

62

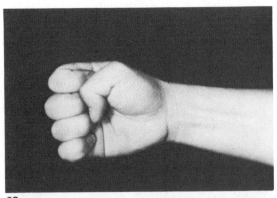

63

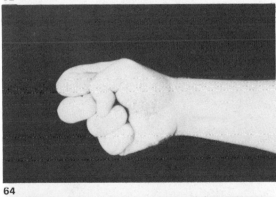

64

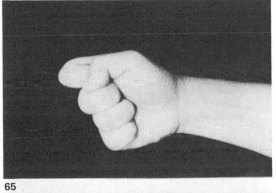

65

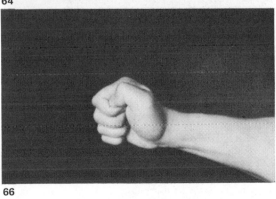

66

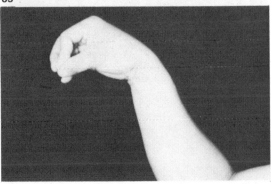

67

45

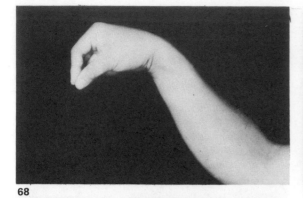

68

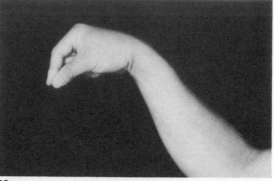

69

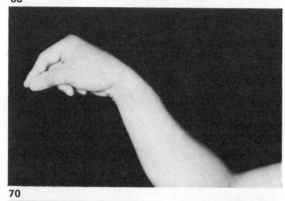

70

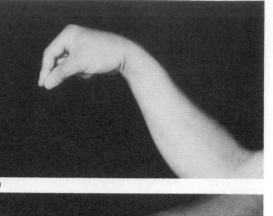

71

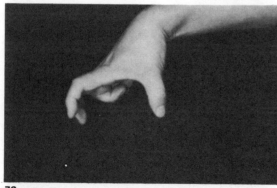

72

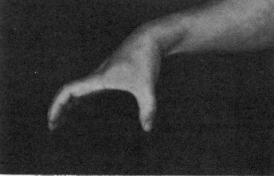

73

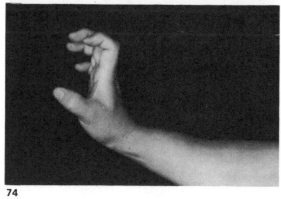

74

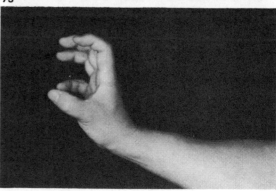

75

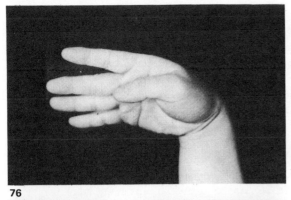

76

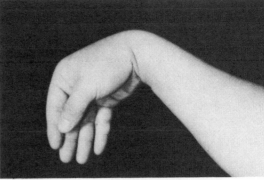

77

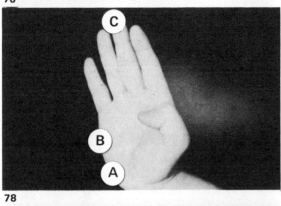

78

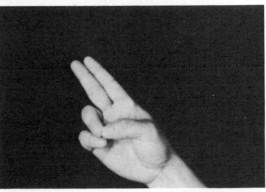

79

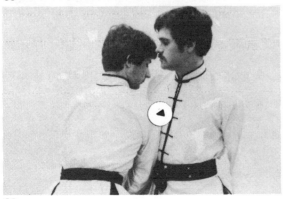

80

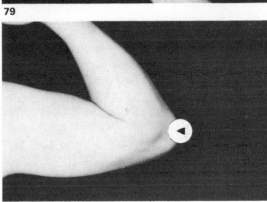

81

82

47

Application of Hand Forms

In the following discussion the martial artist dressed in the black top will be designated "B" while the one in the white top will be "W." In figure 83, W attempts to strike B. As W attacks, B uses his palm (fig. 78) to push away W's elbow while at the same time attacking W's groin with an Eagle Claw (fig. 71) or a Tiger Claw (fig. 75). As an alternative, B may hit W's stomach with a fist (fig. 62). As a footnote to the concept of doors, notice that in figure 83, B has attacked through the right door. Any time an opponent punches he automatically opens the door on the same side of his punch.

In figure 84, as W attempts to punch, B can use a White Crane Wing (fig. 76) to block. In order to expose W's cavities, B covers and pushes down W's hand using the White Crane Wing as shown in figure 85. Once B has pressed down W's hand, B can use an Eagle Claw or Tiger Claw to grab W's throat (fig. 86). As alternatives, B can use a White Crane Wing or a White Crane Beak (fig. 69) to sting the eyes (figs. 87, 88), a Hammer Hand (fig. 63) to strike the eye bridge, or a fist to strike the chin (figs. 89, 90).

In terms of strategy it is extremely useful to block and push a punch down or sideways as B has done in figures 87 and 89. The first advantage is that the opponent loses the immediate use of his right hand for attack. Usually the left hand is too far away to counter, especially if the opponent has his right leg forward. The second advantage is that by blocking with the left, B's right hand is free for a short range attack. Such a short range punch is usually more difficult to block.

In all the examples cited, it has been the left arm which blocks. However, the right hand shaped as a White Crane Wing is also extremely effective for blocking. In using the White Crane Wing to block a punch, the forearm (fig. 80) must first be used to stop the opponent's hand (fig. 91). This is immediately followed with the White Crane Wing over the hand as in figure 92. In figure 92, notice the left hand is at the side of the right forehand; in that position the left can take over and push the opponent's hand down or up, freeing the right hand for punching. In the White Crane division this two-handed method of cooperative blocking is called the "mother-son hand."

83

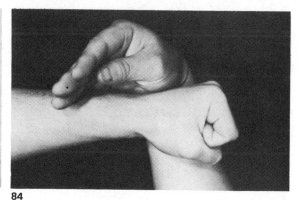

84

85

86

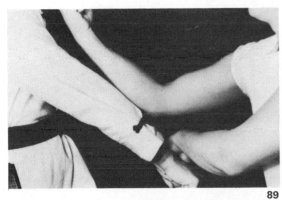

87

88

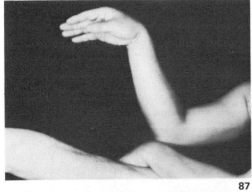

89

90

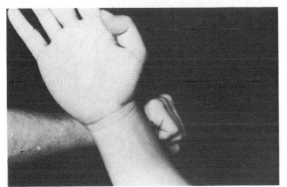

91

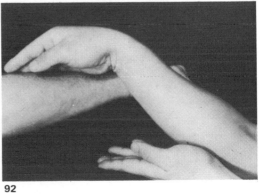

92

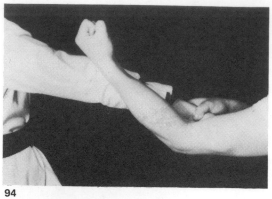

93　94

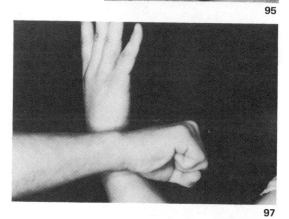

95　96

97　98

99　100

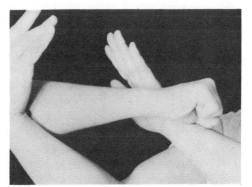

101　**102**

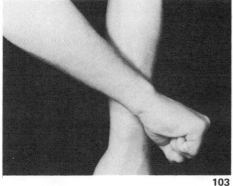

103　**104**

In figure 93, B is blocking with his right hand, using a White Crane Wing. At this point B can grab W's wrist and step forward to break W's elbow with a forearm (fig. 94). If B blocks with his left hand using a White Crane Wing, he can easily grab W's hand and attack the head (fig. 95) or the back (fig. 96). The White Crane Wing is also useful for blocking punches from an inside position as in figures 97 and 98. From this position B can use an elbow on the chest (fig. 99) or a White Crane Beak or Wing to the eyes. Other uses of the White Crane Wing include a block against low strikes (figs. 100, 101) and as a lock on an opponent's punch (fig. 102). Finally, in figures 103 and 104, the forearm is demonstrated to block low punches.

Hand Techniques On A Sandbag

The most practical and basic piece of equipment for practicing power, speed, accuracy, and stability is the kicking or punching bag. In Chinese Wu Su, this bag is filled with sand and is more difficult to practice on because it is heavier and harder than other types of bags, which are usually filled with sawdust or some other softer substance. However, in this volume we will show all hand techniques on a regular type of kicking bag.

In this volume only the techniques for one sandbag are shown, although it is common for some martial artist to use two, three, four, or up to twelve sandbags for their training. For example, during certain stages in the development of the Iron Sand Hand, sandbags of various sizes and weights play important roles.

When training with the kicking bag the student should closely follow these important points:

1. Warm up before any punching practice; the muscles should be loose and warm. When the practice has finished it is necessary to relax the muscles. This can be done by doing the warm-up exercise shown in figure 10.

2. Use the waist to generate punching power. To generate waist power, jerk the waist slightly ahead of every punch. Because waist power can injure the internal organs, it is necessary for the student to wear a snug belt around his midsection during any punching practice.

3. The beginning student must first condition his hands. For the first two weeks only hit the kicking bag with weak or moderate force until the nerves in the hand are conditioned. If the student uses full force at the very beginning, he will over-stimulate his nerves and cause injury through internal bruises.

4. After every session with the kicking bag, soak the hands in hot water while massaging the joints. This type of training usually creates bruises in the hand—the hot water and massage spread the bruises so the body can heal them more quickly and efficiently.

5. Concentrate on the point of the strike. By staring and focusing on one point, more power can be generated. In addition, accuracy is trained.

6. The student must relax. By tensing up, the muscles contract and interfere with movement. Also the student should not hold his breath during practice.

7. The punching arm should be relaxed and loose until the point of impact; at impact the hand and arm is stiffened. By stiffening the hand before impact, the student will avoid wrist and hand injury.

8. Practice every punch without a sandbag to develop the concentration of power in addition to its penetration.

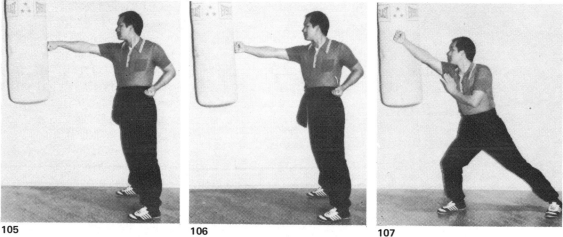

105   106   107

1. **Pin Chuan — "Flat Punch"** (fig. 105; hand form, fig. 62)

   Stand in front of the bag within reaching distance. Both feet should be parallel at shoulder width with the fists at the waist (palms up). When the fist strikes the bag the shoulder should be turned. By turning the shoulders the body forms a triangle which helps in generating waist power while also extending the reach of the fist. Right before impact the fist should spin 180 degrees in order to produce penetration power. This punch usually is used to attack the chest area.

2. **Li Chuan — "Vertical Punch"** (fig. 106; hand form, fig. 62)

   The same as above except the fist only spins 90 degrees. This punch is used to attack the sternum.

3. **Bon Chuan — "Backside of the Hand Punch"** (fig. 107; hand form, fig. 62)

   Stand Deng San Bu with the fist held across the waist. Jerk the waist and swing the fist up. The opposite hand should protect the chest. This punch is used to attack the jaw or temple.

108   **109**   **110**

4. **Sha Bon Chuan — "Back of the Hand Forward Punch"** (fig. 108; hand form, fig. 62)

   Same as Bon Chuan except the fist strikes downward from the waist. Attacks the stomach, side of waist, and groin.

5. **Fan Sou Chuan — "Reverse Hand Punch"** (fig. 109; hand form, fig. 62)

   Stand Deng San Bu with the left fist beside the waist. Jerk the waist and spin the fist 270 degrees so the back of the hand strikes the bag from the side. This punch is used to attack the head, temple, or jaw.

6. **Zuan Sou Chuan — "Spin Punch"** (fig. 110; hand form, fig. 62)

   Same as Fan Sou Chuan except that the fist is used to strike forward. This punch is used to attack the face.

111   **112**   **113**

7. **Chuai Sou — "Hammer Hand"** (fig. 111; hand form, fig. 63)

   Stand Deng San Bu with the right hand behind the ear and left hand protecting the chest. Strike straight forward. This form is used for short range and must be pulled back as quickly as possible. This punch is used to attack the eye bridge, upper lip, or throat.

8. **Shoun Sou Chuan — "Double Hand Punch"** (fig. 112; hand form, fig. 62)

   Stand Deng San Bu with both fists at waist. Spin both fists 270 degrees before impact, thus striking the bag from the side. This can also be done using one hand; in this case it is called a Detour Hook. The hand form for the Detour Hook is figure 66. This punch is used to attack the temple or jaw.

9. **Nei Hen Zou — "Inside Forearm Strike"** (fig. 113; hand form, fig. 80)

   Stand Deng San Bu with both fists at waist. Swing the arm to the side and strike with the inside of the forearm. The fist can also be used for striking. This punch is used to attack the waist, kidney, or elbow.

114   115   116

10. **Sou Dau — "Hand Knife"** (fig. 114; hand form, fig. 78B)

Stand Deng San Bu with the left hand behind the ear and the right hand in front of the chest. Strike at the bag with the left hand while turning the palm 180 degrees so that the side of the hand *hits* and slides: it is important that the hand slides after the strike. This punch is used to attack the neck.

11. **Hen Chieh — "Side Cut"** (fig. 115; hand form, figs. 78B, 80)

Stand Deng San Bu with the right hand held across the waist (palms down). Jerk the waist and strike the bag from the side with the edge of the palm or forearm. This punch is used to attack the waist.

12. **Shan Fan Sou — "Side Upper Strike"** (fig. 116; hand form, fig. 80)

The same as Hen Chieh except the strike is upward and the outside edge of the hand or forearm is used. This punch is used to attack the jaw.

117   118   119

13. **Tuei Chang — "Palm Strike"** (fig. 117; hand form, fig. 78A)

Stand in Ma Bu with both palms open and facing up. Strike out and hit the bag with the lower edge of the palm. The finger tips can be slightly curled. This punch is used to attack the chest.

14. **Shoun Tuei Chang — "Double Palm Strike"** (fig. 118; hand form, fig. 78A)

Same as Tuei Chang except both palms strike out at the same time.

15. **Zou Den — "Elbow Strike"** (fig. 119; hand form, fig. 81)

Stand in Ma Bu with the arms in front of the chest. Jerk the waist and strike the bag with the elbow. This punch is used to attack the chest or shoulder blade.

120   121   122

16. **Whye Hen Zou — "External Forearm Slide Strike"** (fig. 120; hand form, figs. 78, 80)

Stand in Ma Bu with hands at waist. Swing the arm from the side and strike and slide with the edge of the palm or the forearm. This punch is used to attack the stomach or waist.

17. **Pie Chang — "Palm Slap"** (fig. 121; hand form, fig. 78)

Stand in Ma Bu with both hands at waist. Slap the side of the bag with the center of the palm. This punch is used to attack the ear.

18. **Gen Den — "Shoulder Hit"** (fig. 122; hand form, fig. 82)

Stand Deng San Bu and strike bag with shoulder. This punch is used to attack the chest.

LEG TECHNIQUES

Leg Forms

There are only a few parts of the leg which are used for attacking or blocking in all Wu Su divisions. Below are listed the zones of the foot commonly used.

Table 2 Leg Forms

Figure	Name	Zone(s) Used
123	*Tie* ("Kick")	Toe
124	A. *Teng* ("Heel Kick")	Heel
	B. *Den* ("Press")	Bottom front of the foot
	C. *Chiao Hou Gan* ("Back Heel")	Back heel
	D. *Kou* ("Hook")	Front ankle joint
125	*Chieh* ("Cut")	Edge of foot
126	*Shao* ("Sweep")	Bottom of foot
127	A. *Shi* ("Knee")	Knee
	B. *Tuei Jai* ("Shin Block")	Shin
128	*Tun Den* ("Hip Bump")	Hip

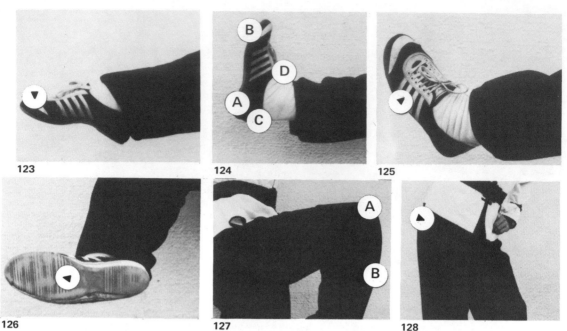

123   124   125

126   127   128

Kicking Techniques

As was mentioned in "Common Knowledge," Northern styles through the years have evolved kicking as their specialty. With the development of kicking skills the Northern, as well as Southern, divisions have found through experience that effective kicking techniques follow a general set of principles. The first and most important rule is not to expose the groin area during the act of kicking. For this reason, Chinese martial artists will usually kick low to areas like the ankle, knee, and groin; in these cases, kicking low does not expose the groin. In addition to affording protection, low kicks are faster, more stable, and usually more effective in free fighting.

Wu Su practitioners, in order to protect their groin, will also not use single high kicks while one leg is touching or planted on the ground. A quick opponent can easily strike the groin while the leg is lifted high. To attack high regions such as the chest or head, the Northern and Southern stylists will usually use a double jump kick. When the martial artist is jumping, the leg that is not kicking is bent and close to the body so that the groin is protected.

Even though Wu Su practitioners kick low in real fighting, during training they will practice their kicks as high as possible. They do this for a special reason: if a person can kick high with speed and power, the low version of that kick will be even more powerful because it is easier to perform. For this reason some of the kicks on the bag will be shown in their high versions.

Listed below are other vital points the student should follow while practicing kicks:

1. Always be stable. Stability (except for jump kicks) involves two important considerations:
   a. While one leg is used for kicking, the other leg should be planted flat and firm on the ground. Figures 130 and 131 are examples of this. *Never* raise the heels of the planted or stable leg while kicking. Only in this way is stability approached and maintained.
   b. During the kick do not twist the hip, and turn or slide the leg which is planted flat. The student may turn the leg or twist the hip in order to get into the proper position before the kick. But once the kick starts no motion is allowed.

2. Kicking power must come from the jerking of the waist, in addition to the leg and hip muscles.
3. After every kick withdraw the leg as quickly as possible. By a quick return of the kicking leg the martial artist cuts down the time he is exposed or vulnerable.
4. Stretch before kicking.
5. Stay relaxed and concentrate on the striking point.
6. Practice every kick using both legs.
7. Practice every kick without a kicking bag. Practicing without a bag is equally important for developing speed, penetration power, and accuracy.
8. Do not hold your breath while kicking.

The following are 26 fundamental and advanced kicks:

129   130   131

132   133   134

1. **Ti Twe — "Toe Kick"** (Figs. 129, 130; leg form, fig. 123)
   Stand Deng San Bu and bring the back leg up so the knee is held near the waist (fig. 129). Quickly snap out the leg so the foot hits the bag flat. The toe is used to kick the groin.
2. **Teng Twe — "Heel Kick"** (figs. 129, 131; leg form, fig. 125)
   This kick is the same as Ti Twe, except use the heel to strike the opponent. The target areas are the groin, abdomen, or chest.

3. **Chei Twe — "Cut Kick"** (figs. 129, 132; leg form, fig. 125)

This kick is the same as Ti Twe and Teng Twe, except the outside edge of the foot is used to strike. Before kicking it may be necessary to turn the stationary leg to get a better kicking angle. But remember, do not turn or twist while kicking. The target areas are the knees, stomach, or chest.

4. **Chan Ding — "Forward Press Kick"** (figs. 129, 133; leg form, fig. 124B)

This kick is the same as Ti Twe except the ball of foot is used. When the kick makes contact it should press forward. The target areas are the chest or stomach.

5. **Tseh Ding — "Side Press Kick"** (figs. 129, 134; leg form, fig. 124B)

Lift the leg and swing it in a semi-circle and hit the side of the bag with the ball of the foot. Again, the student may adjust his legs before the kick, but once the kick begins do not twist or turn the legs and hips. This kick can attack the portion of the body under the arms, waist, or back.

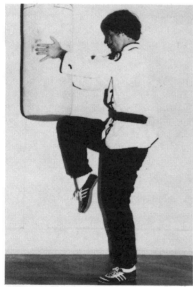

135

136

137

6. **Shi Ding — "Knee Press Kick"** (fig. 135; leg form, fig. 127A)

Stand Deng San Bu and bring the back leg up and hit the bag with the knee. The knee should come up at a 45 degree angle. Target areas are groin or abdomen. When this kick is used in a jump, the target areas are the chin or chest.

7. **Whye Bie — "External Sweep"** (fig. 136; leg form, fig. 125)

To begin, stand with feet parallel with the right leg lightly touching the ground. Bring the right leg up and to the left side of the body in a clockwise motion. When the foot reaches its highest point (directly in front and above the student's left shoulder) swing the leg straight across the body toward the right. Do not raise the heel of the stationary leg. The student is circumscribing a circle in front of his body going from left to right. The strike is made with the side of the foot. This kick is used for attacking the arms or the back: it can also be used for blocking.

8. **Nei Bie — "Internal Sweep"** (fig. 137; leg form, fig. 126)

Stand Deng San Bu with left leg back. Swing the left leg up in a clockwise motion and strike the bag with the bottom of the foot. The leg should swing out fairly wide. As the student kicks the bag he should also slap it with the opposite hand. This kick attacks the back or chest; it can also be used for blocking.

138   139

9. **Shao Twe — "Sweep Kick"** (fig. 138, leg form, fig. 126)

This kick is the same as Nei Bie except that the striking area is lower and the hand does not slap. Shao Twe is used for kicking the calf or knee.

10. **Tseh Tie — "Side Kick"** (fig. 139; leg form, fig. 123)

Bring the leg up and swing it to the side, striking the bag with the instep. The student may adjust his legs before the kick, but he must remain stable during the kick. This kick attacks the area under the arms or the stomach.

140   141   142

11. **Hou Teng Twe — "Back Heel Kick"** (figs. 140, 141; leg form, fig. 124A)

Stand Deng San Bu with the left leg forward and the hands protecting the chest. Before the kick, bring the right leg forward with knee raised (fig. 140). Kick forward using the bottom of the foot or heel to strike while looking back at the opponent or bag. This kick is used to attack the chest or stomach.

12. **Ma Twe — "Horse Kick"** (fig. 142; leg form, fig. 124C)

Stand Deng San Bu with the left leg forward. Sweep the rear leg in a circle until it is in front of the left leg. At this point, kick up with the heel while looking back. This kick is used to attack the groin.

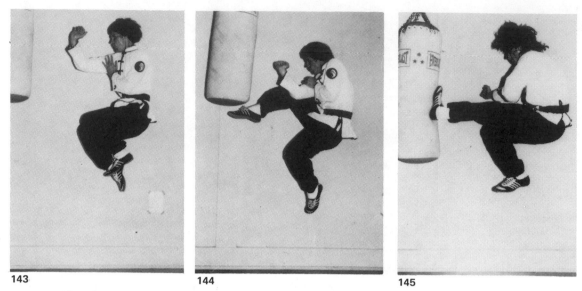

143   144   145

13. Tiao Ti Twe — "Double Jump Kick" (figs. 143, 144; leg form, fig. 123)

This is a double jump kick. Stand Ssu Lieu Bu with both hands protecting the chest. Shift the weight to the front leg and jump forward at the same time kicking Ti Twe with the back leg; figure 143 shows the back leg about to kick. Immediately bring the rear leg to the body and kick the front leg also using Ti Twe (fig. 144). The first kick attacks the groin area while the second kick goes to the chin.

14. Tiao Teng Twe — "Jump Heel Kick" (fig. 145; leg form, fig. 124A)

This kick is the same as Tiao Ti Twe except the second kick is Teng Twe for attacking the chest.

146   147

15. Tiao Nei Bie — "Internal Jump Kick" (fig. 146; leg form, fig. 126)

This kick is the same as Tiao Ti Twe, except the second kick is Nei Bie. Nei Bie should go to the back or face. Sometimes the second kick can block a weapon.

16. Tiao Tseh Chei Twe — "Side-Cut Jump Kick" (fig. 147; leg form, fig. 125 or 126)

This is a single jump kick. Stand Ssu Lieu Bu. Jump off the front leg and bring the knee of the rear leg to the chest and turn slightly sideways while in the air. As the body turns, kick out with the front leg using the edge or bottom of the foot. Strike the stomach, chest, or throat.

148   149

17. Shain Fon Twe — "Tornado Kick" (figs. 148, 149; leg form, fig. 126)

Stand Ssu Lieu Bu with the left leg forward and with both hands protecting the chest. Shift all the weight on the front left leg and spin 270 degrees clockwise (fig. 148). At this point jump straight up and swing the left leg from the outside to the inside (Nei Bie) striking the bag (fig. 149). The bottom of the foot should be used for striking. For kicking with the opposite leg, right and left are switched; in addition, the turn must be counterclockwise. Shain Fon Twe is used for long range attacks to the upper body.

150   151

18. Tiao Hou Teng Twe — "Rear Jump Spin Heel Kick" (figs. 150, 151; leg form, fig. 126)

Stand Ssu Lieu Bu with the right leg forward. Jump off the right leg and spin 180 degrees clockwise (counterclockwise if the left is forward) so that your back is facing the bag. While jumping, both knees should be drawn up near the waist (fig. 150). When the body is turned away from the bag, lean slightly forward and strike out with the right leg (fig. 151). Hit the bag with the bottom of the foot. This kick attacks the stomach or chest.

152   153   154   155

19. Lieu Twe — "Ramble Kick" (fig. 152; leg form, fig. 124B)

Stand Deng San Bu with both hands protecting your chest. Swing the back leg up in a semi-circle straight to the head. At the same time, put the arm which is on the same side of the kick down to protect the groin. This kick is used for attacking the groin and chin.

20. Ma Hou Teng Twe — "Horse Back Heel Kick" (fig. 153; leg form, fig. 124A)

Stand Ma Bu and drop both hands to the floor. When the hands touch the floor kick both feet back. The purpose of Ma Hou Teng Twe is to kick to the rear. This kick is used to attack the chest or belly.

21. Ba Bu Gan Chan — "Eight Steps to Chase the Cicada" (figs. 154, 155; leg form, fig. 125)

Stand Ssu Lieu Bu with both arms protecting the chest. Jump forward, bringing both knees close to the chest (fig. 154). As the student comes down he kicks out with the bottom or edge of the front leg. This kick attacks the knee or ankle.

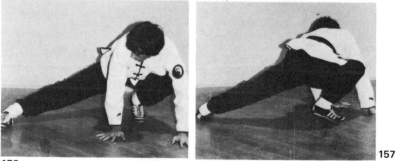

156   157

22. Shao Tan Twe — "Floor Sweep Kick" (figs. 156, 157; leg form, figs. 124C, 124D)

Stand Ssu Lieu Bu with the left leg forward and both hands protecting the chest. Drop down into Fu Hu Bu and swing the right leg across the floor in a counterclockwise direction while shifting the weight onto the left leg (fig. 156). When the right leg is facing the front, shift the weight onto it and swing the left leg counterclockwise across the floor (fig. 157). Repeat again swinging the right leg in a semicircle. The sweep attacks the front leg of an opponent.

158

159

160

161

162

163

23. **Shuang Chao Teng — "Both Leg Kicks"** (fig. 158; leg form, fig. 124A)

Stand in Ma Bu and jump up bringing both knees to the chest. When the knees are in position, kick out Teng Twe with both legs at a 60 degree angle while punching with both arms. This is a simultaneous attack against two opponents. The attack area is the stomach or chest.

24. **Chai Twe — "Step on Kick"** (fig. 159; leg form, fig 124A)

As an opponent attacks, the martial artist blocks the punch and kicks the knee using the heel. The foot should be at a 45 degree angle. This kick is a low form of Teng Twe except that the foot is not at a 90 degree angle to the ground.

25. **Chao Twe — "Hook Kick"** (figs. 160, 161; leg form, fig. 124D)

This kick is used for tripping an opponent. As an opponent punches, the martial artist uses his right hand to block and grasp the opponent while the other hand pushes against the neck (fig. 160). Simultaneous with the block, the martial artist steps forward to kick and hook the opponent's heel (fig. 161). By kicking out the heel and pushing the face, the opponent will fall.

26. **Hou Chai Twe — "Back Split Kick"** (figs. 162, 163; leg form, fig. 124C)

As the opponent punches, the martial artist blocks and steps forward with the right leg (fig. 162). When the block is complete, he slides his right leg back against the opponent's leg (fig. 163). During the trip, the left leg is shuffled forward. When the right leg slices against the opponent's leg, the opponent will be knocked off balance.

POWER AND SPEED TRAINING

Although the practitioners of Chinese Wu Su realize that perfecting the techniques is of the utmost importance, they also realize that every technique must also have speed and power. It is easy to see how an extremely fast and powerful martial artist who has poor technique may overcome a weaker and slower martial artist who has good technique. Every effective technique must and should be fast, powerful, and accurate in form. Therefore, along with the constant practice of technique, there should also be consistent practice of speed and power.

In training for speed and power, it is important to develop both aspects together. The human body contains two types of muscle cells; those that are mainly used for power and those that are mainly used for speed. Therefore, training both speed and power will make the martial artist more efficient with his techniques. Neglecting either power or speed may result in a martial artist who is powerful but slow, or a martial artist who is fast but weak. Neither situation is desirable.

Every Wu Su style has developed its own special training exercises for speed and power. While the particular exercises are different, the purpose and goal is the same. The training methods usually build up the power and speed of all the major areas of the body: hands, arms, shoulders, eyes (speed), and legs. Additionally, there are methods to train mental reaction, dodging, escaping, and withdrawal. The training methods may range from a single individual performing an exercise, to exercises where partners are engaged against each other.

While the training methods for speed and power vary greatly, some aspects are trained no matter what the exercise. First, any time a martial artist performs a drill, he is building up his mental reaction. By doing drills that require quick and powerful movements, the martial artist is building up the quickness of his mind. In time, the student will begin to react naturally, instinctively, and without hesitation; to fight in this manner is the goal of every martial artist. Second, by practicing certain drills with various partners, the student gains experience. By having experience the student can react more quickly and instinctively.

The following training methods are organized so that various important aspects are trained. The drills, if practiced faithfully and diligently, should improve overall speed and power without neglecting any major areas that are necessary for a martial artist. The martial artist does not have to do every drill in every section; instead, he should pick one or two from every section to insure a good balance.

Hands and Fingers

To be proficient in such things as blocking, grabbing, hooking, locking, and Chin Na techniques, it is necessary to have adequate hand and finger speed and strength. In divisions which make great use of the hands for grabbing and clasping, such as White Crane, Eagle Claw, Tiger, and Praying Mantis, drills which improve the speed and power of the hands and fingers are of major importance. Because every division has some techniques which require grabbing, hooking, or clasping, there will exist some drills for improving the hands and fingers.

A good method to develop quick and powerful grasping is to alternately drop and catch a heavy object such as a brick. The brick should not be allowed to touch the ground. When the brick is released, move both hands above the head and then quickly lower them to catch the brick. To make this drill more difficult, and hence increase speed, attempt to clap the hands between one and three times before catching the brick. As proficiency improves, a heavier brick can be used. But before going on to heavier bricks, the martial artist should at least start with one weighing about thirty pounds. In

164

165

166

167

168

earlier times a jar filled with sand was used. As the student got better, more sand was added to the jar.

Doing push-ups is another way to improve the hands and fingers. But instead of using the palms to support the weight of the body, the fingers should be used. As the push-ups are done, the student should attempt to clap his hands one, two, or three times (figs. 164, 165). Speed and power will both be trained in this drill.

In White Crane, Eagle Claw, and Tiger, a common way to build up grasping power is a method called grasping empty air. This section will show the Eagle Claw and Tiger methods. To begin, assume Ma Bu with the fists at the waist. Swing the right hand up so that fingers are pointing up as in figure 166. By swinging the hand up, an imaginary punch is blocked from the inside position. Next, point the fingers forward in the form of an eagle claw (fig. 167) and slowly clench it while concentrating on generating power. Return the right hand to the waist and punch forward with the left fist while turning the hips 90 degrees clockwise to assume Deng San Bu as in figure 168. This action represents the martial artist grabbing the blocked punching arm of the imaginary opponent and countering with his own punch. After punching, turn 90 degrees counterclockwise and reassume Ma Bu, while opening the left fist and turning the fingers up. Next, point the fingers forward, form an eagle claw, pull back the left arm and punch with the right fist while turning the hips 90 degrees counterclockwise into Deng San Bu. Return to the original position and begin the whole process over with the extended right hand. White Crane uses basically the same method except a White Crane Wing is used instead of an Eagle Claw.

169

170

171

172

The Tiger division version of grasping empty air is called Bai Bar Chuar or "one-hundred grasps." To begin, stand in Ma Bu. Strike out with both palms facing forward as in figure 118. With each hand, make two small circles; the right hand moves clockwise and the left hand moves counterclockwise; both hands should cross each other as in figure 169. Turn the palms out as in figure 170 while making a Tiger Claw. Slowly clench the Tiger Claw while concentrating on power; the forearm and hand should be at about a 90 degree angle. Return both hands to the waist and begin again.

A final way to improve grasping is to quickly make as many fists as possible within a 30 second period. The hand alternately must be completely open and completely closed (figs. 171, 172). The martial artist should attempt to make 180 fists in 30 seconds, or 5 fists per second.

Wrist, Arms, Shoulders

Once an opponent is grabbed, it will require wrist and arm power to adequately control him. Wrist and arm power must complement the power in the hand and fingers. A simple way to build such overall power is to hold a rod near its center and move it up and down while keeping the arm relatively stationary at the side. Later, the martial artist can hold the rod more toward one end to increase the difficulty of the drill. Another way is to hold a rod near the center and move it up and down from a fixed center as in figure 173. The arm holding the rod should be straight.

In White Crane the stylists commonly use wooden rods or several bamboo poles to build up the wrist and arms. One method using wooden rods begins with the partners holding the rods in tandem and as tightly as possible. Both partners simultaneously swing the rods down and up in a clockwise arc as in figure 174. When the rods reach the opposite position, swing them down and up, back to the starting position. As the partners on each side swing the rods, the rods will be twisted. To keep the original tandem position, both martial artists must hold tightly. A variation of this same drill is for one side to remain motionless while the other spins his body clockwise or counterclockwise as in figure 175. The side that loses the tandem grip is the loser.

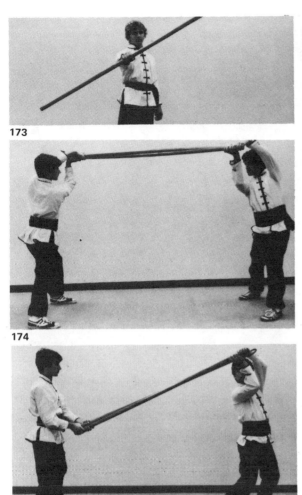

173

174

175

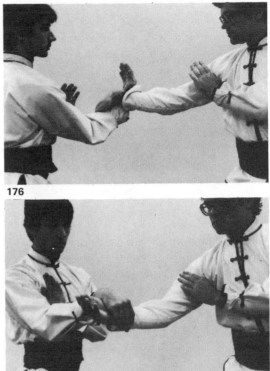

176

177

A more difficult drill which improves the wrist, arm, and shoulder is to stick two large bamboo poles in the ground, about two feet apart, and attempt to climb up while grasping each pole. To increase the power needed, the martial artist should grease or soap his hands.

A very important method in White Crane for developing the arms for Chin Na techniques is "rubbing hand" or *Mou Sou*. To begin, two students face each other with their right legs forward. Next, one person forms a White Crane Wing with the right hand and hooks it over the right wrist of the other person; the student who has his wrist hooked should have his palm facing inward and his fingers pointed up (fig. 176). For convenience, the martial artist who has his hand originally hooked will be called A; the one originally performing the hook will be called B. The goal of A is to get his wrist unhooked while also hooking B's wrist. To do this A must jerk his arm back using waist power. Once A has pulled B's arm back sufficiently, he can hook B's wrist as in figure 177. But as A is attempting to jerk back B's wrist, B will himself be jerking back to prevent A from hooking; this is why A cannot rehook B's wrist in figure 176. Both sides can easily feel when the White Crane Wing has been applied. When the hook has been successfully applied, the other side must turn his hands up as A in figure 176. This drill must be done without stopping—each side is constantly attempting to get free or maintain the hook.

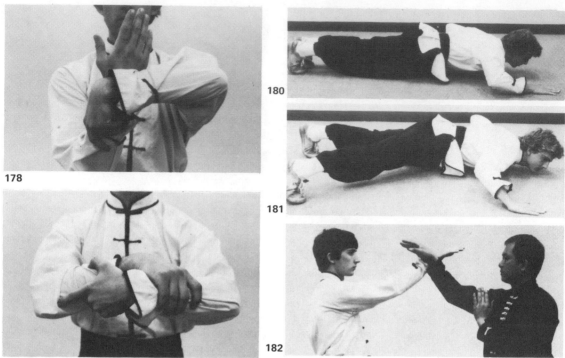

178

179

180

181

182

If no partner is immediately available, the student can practice by himself the drill shown in figures 178 and 179. Begin by grabbing the right wrist with the left hand as in figure 178. Swing the right hand inside and grab the left wrist (fig. 179). Next, the left hand moves up and inside to grab the right wrist. Keep repeating this same process. The martial artist should resist himself as much as possible.

A popular way to build upper arm and shoulder strength is to do hand crawling. First, assume the crawling position in figure 180. Starting from this position, the student can move forward, backward, or laterally (fig. 181). But in the process of moving, certain rules should be followed: first, knees must be locked; second, the arms are bent as low as possible without the chest touching the ground; third, only the arms can be used to drag the body along—no assistance can come from the legs. To move the body forward, the student can drag his body or hop off the hands. Moving backward requires either pushing or hopping off the hands. Moving laterally requires that the hands and legs on the same side of the body move together in the same direction.

Eyes and Hands

The best way to train the eyes is to practice with a partner using a fighting form. An example of this is shown in figure 182. Chapter 5 will go into more detail about fighting forms. Both students stand facing each other so that they can reach each other's forehead. One side then tries to attack by touching the forehead of his partner. The defender in turn will try to block the touch by using a White Crane Wing. Each side should assume one role and continuously block or attack for 30 seconds. After 30 seconds the role of attacker and defender is switched. It is very important not to close the eyes during this training. The student must keep his eyes open and get used to fast motion. This method can also be practiced alone in front of a mirror.

A method which is useful for unifying the eyes and mind as one unit, a vital trait in any free fighting, is the practice of gazing at burning incense or a candle for at least five

183   184   185

186   187

minutes. The mind must remain calm and concentrated during the practice. By constant gazing, the eyes and mind become coordinated so any motion can be instantly reacted to.

Stability

The most important trait which the beginning student should develop is stability. Stability is always practiced when a student performs a sequence, but a more common way to build up stability is to stand in Ma Bu. The student should stand in Ma Bu about 5 to 10 minutes; any longer than 10 minutes may injure the knees. While standing in Ma Bu, the student should concentrate on directing the power of his legs straight down. A good way to test whether the student is achieving downward power is to stand Ma Bu on two bricks for 5 to 10 minutes (fig. 183). If the student directs his power to the sides he will fall off the bricks.

Another method of training stability is called "the child worshipping the Buddha" (fig. 184). In this form the student places his hands in a praying position and raises one leg so that it is slightly bent with the bottom of the foot facing out. Stand in this position for at least five minutes. A variation of this is to extend the leg straight (fig. 185) and slowly squat on the supporting leg (fig. 186). The leg which is straight should at no time touch the ground. After squatting, the straight leg swings to the rear of the body (fig. 187). Resume the original position without touching the ground with the lifted leg and repeat the process. Later switch legs.

188   189   190   191

Punching and Kicking

Punching and kicking power can be achieved by several methods outside of using the sandbag. Putting extra weight on the arms or legs while punching or kicking is a good method to improve overall power. A method which is equal in importance to sandbag training is the punching and kicking of the air; punching and kicking air helps to develop the capacity to make one's power penetrate beyond the mere surface attack.

In the Shao Lin Temple, a common way to build up a monk's penetration power was for him to punch or kick a burning candle and attempt to extinguish the flame: this drill is still commonly used. This method, when practiced, requires concentration, penetration power, and relaxation to extinguish the candle. When the student can put out the flame at close range, he should stand further back and attempt to achieve greater levels of penetration power.

To build up punching and kicking speed the student should perform a kick or punch as quickly as he can within a time limit. The student can pick any suitable form from "Hand Techniques" and "Leg Techniques" and do this type of speed training. The time limit should be about 20 to 30 seconds for each form; in addition, the number of kicks and punches in the time period should be counted. Each time a drill is performed the student should try to add one or two extra punches or kicks to the total count.

Power and speed for kicking can be developed by four methods. The first way is to jump as high as possible while raising the knees to their maximum level (fig. 188). This drill develops the muscles necessary for jump kicks. The second method is to run in place raising the knees as high as possible (fig. 189). By running in place, the upper leg muscles are developed so that the legs will have little trouble in being lifted to send off a kick. The third method is to continuously kick Ti Twe by alternating legs; this develops total kicking speed (fig. 190). The last method is to kick as high as possible while touching the leg with the opposite side hand (fig. 191). This drill is done continuously, alternating legs and hands. Every one of these drills should be done as fast as possible within a 10 second time interval.

ATTACKING ZONES

There are four vital areas which every martial artist must learn to defend and attack: they are the head, chest, belly (including the groin) and back. Although these areas are of vital importance for the maintenance of life, some styles neglect to develop defensive techniques to protect them. This problem is made worse by the fact that many martial artists who only train for tournaments (where the attack of the head, groin, and back is forbidden) rarely develop defenses for these vital areas; this lack of knowledge is eventually passed on to their students. In fact, some students are encouraged to turn their backs (a forbidden zone of attack) to an opponent during a tournament to avoid the scoring of a point to the chest.

Before a student learns the specific zones for attack, he should first master blocking, escaping, withdrawal, and dodging techniques. Some schools reject this and claim that attack is the best defense. But what happens when a student encounters an opponent more skilled in attack? The student obviously loses unless he is skilled in defense.

When a martial artist does attack, he always directs his attacks to specific cavities or to specific vital areas such as the eyes, throat, and groin; throwing blind punches to a general area seldom achieves much. While the last three areas are not cavities, they are nevertheless extremely vulnerable. In attacking a cavity, many considerations must be taken into account. The martial artist must know the depth of a cavity, the proper amount of power needed to reach it, the time of day, month, season, or year that the cavity is effective (since Chi circulates in cycles), the results of hitting a cavity, and the type of punch or kick to use. It is not surprising that such dangerous knowledge was considered highly secret and only taught to students of the highest morality.

In Chinese Wu Su there are 108 cavities which have been found useful for attack (acupuncture uses over 700 cavities): 36 are lethal and 72 cause local paralysis, numbness, or loss of consciousness. Even though many divisions keep secret the location of some cavities, the number still remains at no more than 108. In this volume 53 zones (fig. 192 and Table 3) will be located along with such information as the nerve, hand or leg forms necessary to effectively attack the cavity. If the student wishes to find the exact location of the cavities, he can consult the acupuncture books listed at the end of this chapter.

Books on Acupuncture

Austin, Mary. *Acupuncture Therapy*. Asi Publishers, 1972

Chu, David and Dorothy. *The Principles of Chinese Acupuncture Medicine*. Rainbow Printing, 1975

Mann, Felix. *Acupuncture: The Ancient Chinese Art of Healing and How It Works Scientifically*. Random House, 1971

Silverstein, Marin Elliot. *Acupuncture and Moxibustion*. Schochen Books, 1975

Tan, Leong T. *Acupuncture Therapy: Current Chinese Practice, Second Edition*. Temple University Press, 1976

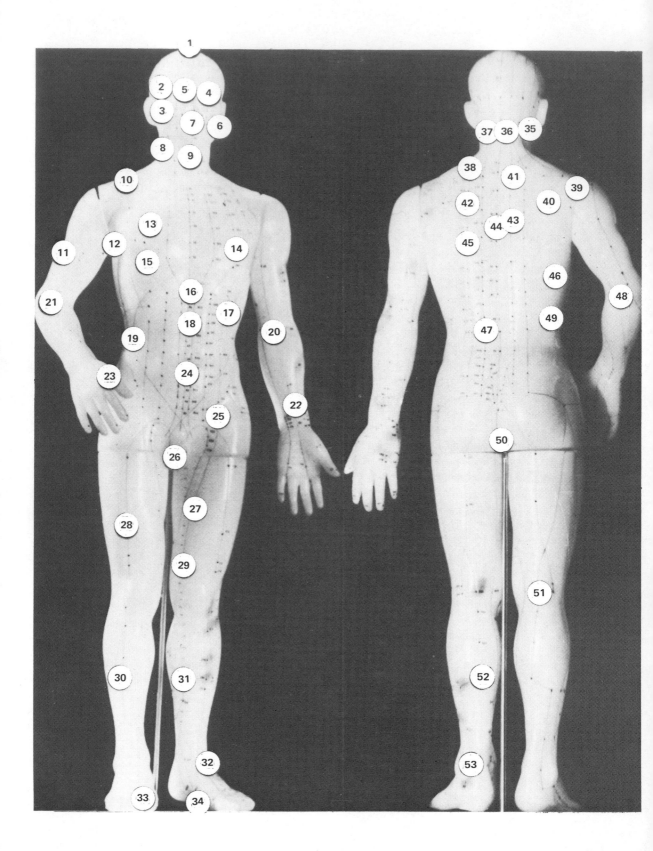

Table 3 ATTACKING ZONES

No.	Chinese Name	English Name	Attack Forms Figure	Result(s)	Nerve System
1	Baihui	Crown of head	121	Death	Governing Vessels Du Mei
2	Taiyang	Temple	64,65,66, 107,109,112	Fainting or death	Stomach Meridian Wei Ching
3	Erhmen	Front of ear	107,109,112, 116,121,136, 137	Fainting or death	Triple Burner Meridian San Chiao Ching
4	Ien	Eyes	67,68,69, 70,76	Blinding	
5	Biliang	Eye bridge	63,111	Fainting or death	Conception Vessels Jen Mei
6	Jiache or Yasha	Side of jaw	107,109,112, 116,136,137	Fainting	Stomach Meridian Wei Ching
7	Zenzhong	Upper lip	63,64,111	Fainting	Conception Vessels Jen Mei
8	Tianchuang or Gencheh	Side of neck	114	Fainting or death	Small Intestine Meridian Shao Chang Ching
9	Lianquan or Ienhou	Throat	63,71,72, 73,74,75,111	Death	Conception Vessels Jen Mei
10	Jugu	Shoulder bone (top)	71,72,73, 74,75	Arm is numb	Large Intestine Meridian Ta Chang Ching
11	Binao	Outside of upper arm	80,113	Arm is numb	Large Intestine Meridian Ta Chang Ching
12	Jiquan	Armpit	79	Death	Heart Meridian Shin Ching
13	Yingchuang or Giantai	Upper pectoral	62,105,117, 118,119	Fainting or death	Stomach Meridian Wei Ching
14	Zuzhong	Nipple	62,105,117, 118,119	Fainting or death	Stomach Meridian Wei Ching
15	Zugen	Lower pectoral	62,105,117, 118,119	Fainting or death	Stomach Meridian Wei Ching
16	Hsinkan	Solar plexus (Sternum)	62,64,106, 117,119,122, 127,131,135, 145,151	Fainting or death	Conception Vessels Jen Mei
17	Qimen	Base of rib	108,113,115, 120,139	Fainting or death	Liver Meridian Kan Ching
18	Zhongwan	Stomach	62,105,106, 131,141,145, 151	Fainting or death	Conception Vessels Jen Mei
19	Zhangmen	Side of waist	108,113,115, 120,132,139, 141	Fainting or death	Liver Meridian Kan Ching
20	Quze	Inside elbow joint	71,72,73, 74,75	Arm is numb	Pericardium Meridian Hsin Pao Ching
21	Quchi	Front side of elbow joint	71,72,73, 74,75,80	Arm is numb	Large Intestine Meridian Ta Chang Ching
22	Neiquan or Wanmei	Inside wrist	71,72,73, 74,75	Arm is numb or fainting	Pericardium Meridian Hsin Pao Ching
23	Hegu or Fukou	Pit of thumb	71,72	Numbness or death	Large Intestine Meridian Ta Chang Ching
24	Qihai or Dantian	Belly	62,105,108, 131,132,133, 141,151	Death	Conception Vessels Jen Mei
25	Chongmen	Front of thigh joint	62,105	Leg is numb	Spleen Meridian Pi Ching
26	Shayin	Groin	71,72,73, 74,75,130, 134,135,142	Death	Liver Meridian Kan Ching

Table 3 ATTACKING ZONES

No.	Chinese Name	English Name	Attack Forms Figure	Result(s)	Nerve System
27	Jimen or Baihai	Inside thigh	131	Fainting	Spleen Meridian Pi Ching
28	Futu	Middle of front thigh	171	Leg is numb	Stomach Meridian Wei Ching
29	Xuehai	Inside and above knee	131,138	Leg is numb	Spleen Meridian Pi Ching
30	Tiaokou	Outside of shin	131,132	Leg is numb	Stomach Meridian Wei Ching
31	Zhongdu	Inside of shin	71,72,126, 138	Leg is numb	Liver Meridian Kan Ching
32	Jiexi	Front of ankle	132,125	Foot is numb	Stomach Meridian Wei Ching
33	Taichong	Pit of big toe	124A	Fainting	Liver Meridian Kan Ching
34	Yongquan	Bottom of foot	71,72	Death	Kidney Meridian Shen Ching
35	Yifeng or Tianzon	Back of ear lobe	64	Fainting or death	Triple Burner Meridian Sanjiao Ching
36	Yamen	Back of neck	78B	Numbness or death	Governing Vessels Du Mei
37	Tianzhu	Muscle of back neck	78B	Fainting or death	Bladder Meridian Pan Kuan Ching
38	Jianjing	Pit of shoulder	64,71,72	Shoulder is numb	Gall Bladder Meridian Tan Ching
39	Naoshu	Back of shoulder joint	63,64	Shoulder is numb	Small Intestine Meridian Shao Chang Ching
40	Tianzong	Center of shoulder blade	64,65	Shoulder is numb or death	Small Intestine Meridian Shao Chang Ching
41	Fongmen or Fonyen	Side of second vertebrae	64	Fainting or death	Bladder Meridian Pan Kuang Ching
42	Gaohuang	Side of upper back	63,64	Fainting or death	Bladder Meridian Pan Kuan Ching
43	Dushu or Zudon	Beside spinal cord	64	Fainting or death	Bladder Meridian Pan Kuang Ching
44	Lingtai or Baihsin	Center of back	62	Fainting or death	Governing Vessels Du Mei
45	Geguan or Fonwye	Under shoulder blade	63,64	Fainting or death	Bladder Meridian Pan Kuang Ching
46	Gienchu	Back side muscle	134	Fainting	
47	Shenshu	Kidney	62,113	Death	Bladder Meridian Pan Kuang Ching
48	Shaohai	Crazy bone	80,113	Arm is numb	Small Intestine Meridian Shao Chang Ching
49	Jingmen or Hsiaoyao	Back of waist	134	Death	Gall Bladder Meridian Dan Ching
50	Changqian or Wyelu	Tail bone	134,135	Death	Governing Vessels Du Mei
51	Weizhong	Knee pit	71,72	Leg is numb	Bladder Meridian Pan Kuang Ching
52	Chengshan or Ghubin	Back of calf	71,72,131	Leg is numb	Bladder Meridian Pan Kuang Ching
53	Kunlun or Gongsun	Back of ankle	71,72	Foot is numb	Bladder Meridian Pan Kuang Ching

74

CHAPTER 3
FUNDAMENTAL SEQUENCES

THEORY

Starting with this chapter and continuing to the next, five Long Fist sequences will be presented. But before going on the martial artist should be aware of some important ideas guiding the construction and performance of sequences. As was mentioned in "Basic Concepts in Wu Su," a sequence is constructed by using a number of techniques—usually ten or more. Each technique, in addition, has a solution. What was mentioned in Chapter 1, but not elaborated on, was the fact that one technique may have two or three solutions; many techniques have several hidden ways of attack and defense not obvious to a person watching. Normally, the first level of solution can be easily picked up by an experienced martial artist while the second and third solutions are more difficult to see. This happens because the second and third level solutions are not performed but are secretly hidden in the first level of solution through the way a hand is held, the positioning of an elbow, a stance, or a number of other ways. The second technique of Lien Bu Chuan (Figs. 6a and b) is a good example of how a second level solution is hidden by a stance. As the student goes through the directions, he should memorize each solution.

When the student begins the practice of sequences, the first consideration he should have is the accuracy and correctness of forms. The offensive and defensive techniques of sequences were designed to maximize the protection of vital zones while affording the best position for further attack or defense. To grossly deviate from the prescribed positions would be to lose the potential effectiveness of the techniques. Besides the practical considerations, when a student is not correct in his forms, the beauty of the sequence is lost. Kung Fu is, after all, a form of art that strives for practical results through a combination of simplicity and complexity, which eventually merges to form the kind of beauty that every painter, writer, and musician seeks a whole lifetime to achieve.

The first consideration in achieving correct and accurate form is proper stance. The stances are especially important because they are the foundation of stability. Every stance which is assumed in Lien Bu Chuan is described in Chapter 2 and must conform as closely as possible to those descriptions; in particular, each stance should be low. A few points which the student must watch that are related to stance and stability are the raising of the heel and the incorrect positioning of the upper body. A common fault among beginning students is the inability to plant the feet stable and flat. Many students, especially in Deng San Bu, will raise the rear foot on its toes. This causes instability and keeps the student from pushing his power forward during punches. Any time a punch is thrown the rear leg must push backward so that a symmetrical relationship is established where backward power equals forward power. With the symmetrical balance of power that is caused by the rear leg pushing back, overall power is increased because more power is thrown forward and the waist becomes more effective in generating jerking power. The other fault is when students do not keep their upper body perpendicular to the ground. By leaning too far foɪward or backward, the student can be pulled forward or pushed backward very easily.

When practicing any sequence it is vitally important that every technique be alive. Every technique is only semi-dead until the student can become familiar enough with it to use in real fighting. Every technique must be practiced with *speed, waist power, stability, reaction,* and *relaxation or calmness* of mind that a real fight would require. Doing the sequence as a mere routine makes it inefficient and dead. The best way to make the sequence alive is to develop a sense of the enemy. This is achieved by constantly imagining that every technique is being performed against a real opponent. The eyes must for this reason continually focus on the enemy as in a real fight.

As each technique of the sequence approaches higher levels of execution, the techniques must also become second nature. The techniques should become accurate, quick, powerful, and spontaneous without the student having to think about every form. This includes such points as always keeping the elbows down to protect the chest, breathing naturally and never holding the breath while punching or kicking, keeping the fingers closed to avoid injury, and keeping a constant sense of the need to protect vital areas while attacking or defending. If the martial artist cannot react naturally, but must remember any part, then he has not even begun to approach elementary levels. Practicing the sequence at least 1,000 times will help develop this second nature.

Lastly, the student should view each technique in a sequence as teaching him general principles of attack or defense. Every sequence can be thought of as a book of formulas which solve different problems. Although each form is precisely prescribed in its detailed movement, the forms have general principles to guide them. For example, in the first technique of Lien Bu Chuan (Fig. 4a), the basic idea is to block an opponent's punch upward in order to expose the lower region—which is then attacked. In the sequence, the actual technique may be thought of as one of the perfect ways to make the idea alive. In a real fight, the martial artist can then apply the formula, changing or altering it to fit the special circumstances of the encounter. Only by constant practice of the technique can the student hope to use the basic idea behind it. Later, as the student develops the technique so that it becomes a habit, he may naturally and quickly react according to the principles of the technique, and not its outer form. A helpful way to get an understanding of the principles behind a technique is to discuss the solutions of the techniques with a partner after practicing the sequence. By constantly probing and researching, the martial artist can gain much that is never explicitly told to him. As in every martial art, the mind must be developed with the body.

In the description of the sequence a few important points must be noted. In Chinese martial books when a sequence is described, a compass system is commonly used to indicate the direction in which the student is facing or moving. This system will be followed in this book. This system is necessary because every picture is taken at the angle which will best reveal the main points of the form. When a student begins a sequence, the direction he is originally facing is always referred to as "N." From this, his right is always and automatically designated "E"; his left then becomes "W." The back is designated "S." As an example, if the change between techniques is from "N" to "W" the student must turn to his left. All the directions which the student must move or face will be in parenthesis. Secondly, some details are omitted for the description because the student can refer to the photographs if he is unsure of any detail. The photographs represent the correct form.

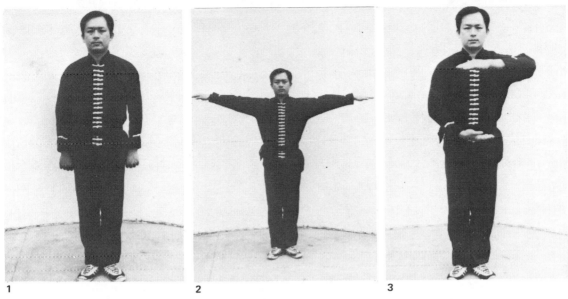

1   2   3

LIEN BU CHUAN

Lien Bu Chuan (the "Continuous Step Sequence") is the first and most fundamental sequence of Long Fist. The basic purpose of this sequence is to familiarize the student with some of the concepts of Long Fist: large and wide postures, continuous movement, approach, withdrawal, and relaxation. The name of the sequence itself, Continuous Step, reflects a basic idea of the constant movement of approach and withdrawal. Although Long Fist specializes in kicking, only two kicks are performed in the sequence. Before effective kicking can be approached the student must first build up his stability and smoothness.

Greeting

  Form: 1, 2, 3 (N). Move the arms straight up with palms facing down. Move the left hand across the chest and the right hand to the belly. In ancient times, Northern Chinese people wore long gowns; therefore, in order to perform a sequence they had to tuck in their gowns so that their legs would not be restricted. These forms represent the tucking in of the gown.

4

5

6

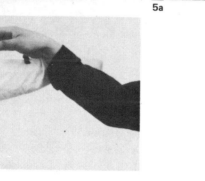

4a

5a

6a

4b

6b

Technique 1

Form: 4, 5 (W). Slide feet 90 degrees counterclockwise and move the right hand up and left hand down while squatting. Step with the left leg into Deng San Bu and cut with the left palm.

Solution: 4A, 4B, 5A. As an opponent throws a punch, the defender blocks up and steps forward to cut the waist. The block may also be in the form of a White Crane Wing.

7 8 9

7a 8a 9a

9b

Technique 2

  Form: 6, 7, 8 (E). Turn 180 degrees clockwise into Sheun Gi Bu while swinging the right hand up; the left hand follows. Push the left hand across body, and withdraw the right hand to the waist. Step forward with the right leg into Deng San Bu while punching with the right hand.

  Solution: 6A, 6B, 7A, 8A. As the opponent punches, the defender swings his right arm to block. The defender's left hand then pushes the opponent's fist away while he steps in to punch the chest. Figure 6B shows a second level solution; after blocking, the defender can kick with the right leg. Notice that this solution is not performed, but is hidden in the sequence.

10

11

12

11a

12a

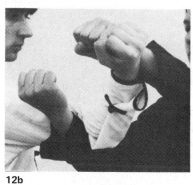

12b

12c

13

14

15

13a

15a

Technique 3

Form: 9, 10 (N). Turn 90 degrees and swing the right arm down and up to shoulder level while raising the left leg. Step down with the left leg into Deng San Bu and cut with the left hand.

Solution: 9A, 9B, 5A (N). As an attacker punches the defender blocks up and steps forward to hit the waist. Figure 9B shows a second level solution; after blocking, step on the knee.

Technique 4

Form: 11 (N). Step forward into Deng San Bu with the right leg, while swinging the left arm in a circle toward the face and punching with the right arm. The elbow must point forward.

Solution: 11A. As an opponent punches, the left hand blocks and the right arm punches.

Technique 5

Form: 12, 13 (N). Turn the right fist up and place the left fist on the right shoulder. Move the right leg back and shift into Sheun Gi Bu while punching down.

Solution: 12A, 12B, 12C, 13A. After blocking a punch, the defender hooks the opponent's arm with his right arm while locking with his left hand. The defender then pushes down with his left hand while pulling with the right. As the defender steps back he can block a kick by striking the leg.

Technique 6

Form: 14 (N). Repeat 11.

Solution: 11A.

16

17

18

16a

17a

18a

18b

Technique 7

Form: 15, 16, 17 (N). Step forward with the left leg into Ssu Lieu Bu while swinging down the left arm. Shift 60 percent of the weight forward into Deng San Bu while striking up with the right palm. Immediately bring the right arm down while swinging the left fist up.

Solution: 15A, 16A, 17A. As an opponent punches, the defender blocks down with his left hand. He then strikes the neck of the opponent and follows this with a fist to the side of the face.

Technique 8

Form: 18 (N). Bring the left leg back and lower the left arm.

Solution: 18A, 18B. The left hand blocks an opponent's punch to the waist. The second level solution is to kick the instep of the attacker after the block.

19

20

21

19a

20a

20b

Technique 9

Form: 19, 20 (N). Step forward with the left leg while making a counterclockwise circle with the left arm. The left palm and foot are facing out. Step with the right leg forward into Ssu Lieu Bu and swing the right forearm into the left palm.

Solution: 19A, 20A, 20B. As the attacker punches, the defender blocks, steps forward and strikes the opponent's elbow with his forearm. A second level solution is to elbow the chest.

22

23

24

22a

23a

24a

Technique 10

Form: 21, 22 (N). Slide the left hand under and up the right arm while stepping forward with the left leg into Ssu Lieu Bu. The left arm is thrust forward once it has gone past the right hand.

Solution: 22A. The defender blocks as the attacker punches.

Technique 11

Form: 23, 24, 25, 26 (N). Swing the left hand down and step forward with the right leg into Deng San Bu; the right hand is above the left hand. Strike forward with the fingers of the right hand. Shift the stance into Ssu Lieu Bu while sliding the left hand up and under the right arm. The right hand retreats to the waist and the left hand forms a fist. Shift into Ma Bu and punch to the side.

Solution: 23A, 24A, 25A, 26A. After blocking down, the defender steps into the opponent and attacks the eyes. If the opponent blocks the sting to the eyes, the defender grabs the blocking hand (fig. 25A) and punches.

Technique 12

Form: 27, 28 (S). Turn the body counterclockwise to S. At the same time, shift into Deng San Bu and move the right arm down and up. Simultaneously, move the left hand in front of the body, and then on to the right shoulder. Move the left leg back into Sheun Gi Bu while sliding the left hand down right arm.

Solution: 27A. The defender blocks the opponent's punch and slaps his palm into the enemy's groin. By shifting back into Sheun Gi Bu the groin can be pulled and attacked simultaneously.

25

26

27

25a

26a

27a

28

29

30

Technique 13
    Form: 29 (S). Same as 18.
Solution: 18A, 18B.

31

32

33

31a

32a

33a

Technique 14

Form: 30, 31 (S). Repeat 19 and then swing the right arm in a circle over the head and strike down into the left palm. Right leg is forward in Deng San Bu.

Solution: 19A, 31A. After blocking a punch, the defender strikes the head of the opponent.

Technique 15

Form: 32, 33, 34 (S). Raise the right leg and arm simultaneously. Bring the right arm straight down while swinging the left arm down in front of the body until it is in position 33; the left hand is under the right fist. Step forward with the right leg into Deng San Bu and attack with the fingers of the right hand.

34

35

36

35a

36a

Solution: 32A, 33A, 24A. As an opponent punches, the right hand blocks up. The defender then pulls the attacker's arm down with his right hand while the left hand covers. The defender then pokes or stings the eyes.

Technique 16

Form: 35 (N), 36 (E), 37 (E). Turn the body counterclockwise so the body faces N; the stance is Deng San Bu. As you turn, bring the right hand across the body so its forearm is perpendicular to the ground; the left hand is under the right arm. The face must be pointing S while executing this move. Slide the left hand up the right arm while clenching the fist. Once the left fist is past the right arm, swing the right arm down in a fist. The stance is Ma Bu in 36 and 37.

Solution: 35A, 36A, 37A. With the right hand, the defender blocks a punch. His left hand then slides up to grab the opponent's arm while his right hand strikes down.

37

38

39

37a

Technique 17
> **Form:** 38, 39 (S). Step forward with the left leg into Ssu Lieu Bu while bringing hands to chest. Repeat 22.

Technique 18
> **Form:** 40 (S). Repeat 18.
> **Solution:** 18A, 18B.

Technique 19
> **Form:** 41, 42 (S). Repeat 19 and 31.
> **Solution:** 19A, 31A.

Technique 20
> **Form:** 43 (S). Bring the right hand down and strike up with the left palm. Do not shift your stance.
> **Solution:** 43A. As the opponent attempts to punch, the right hand blocks down while the left hand cuts the neck.

Technique 21
> **Form:** 44 (E), 45 (N), 46 (N). Leaving the left hand extended, begin to turn counterclockwise. When facing completely N, shift into Deng San Bu (left leg forward), reach forward with the left hand and make a hooking motion with it. After this, throw the right forearm into the left hand.
> **Solution:** 45A, 46A. As the left hand swings back it blocks a punch. Once the punch is blocked, the defender's left hand hooks the neck and the right forearm hits the face.

40

41

42

43

44

45

43a

45a

46

47

48

46a

48a

Technique 22

Form: 47 (N), 48 (S). Bring both arms close to the chest while sliding the left hand over the right fist; the face then turns S. Turn the body to face S and thrust up with the right elbow; the stance is Deng San Bu.

Solution: 48A. The elbow attacks the opponent's chest while the opponent punches.

Technique 23

Form: 49, 50 (W). Turn to the right side and kick Chao Twe while bringing both hands to the side of the head. The back of the hands are turned toward the head as much as possible.

Solution: 49A. As the opponent attempts a double punch to the head, the defender blocks with both hands while kicking Chao Twe to trip the attacker.

Technique 24

Form: 51 (W). Snap into Ma Bu while pushing hands down.

Solution: 51A. This movement blocks the kick to the groin.

49

50

51

49a

51a

52

53

54

52a

53a

Technique 25

Form: 52 (S), 53 (S), 54 (N), 55 (S). Turn S into Deng San Bu and swing the left hand up with the palm facing out. Raise the right leg up and swing the right arm back. Swing the right arm around until it points N while shifting into Deng San Bu; the body is turned to the N while shifting into Deng San Bu; the body is turned to the N while the face is pointing S (fig. 54). Turn the body clockwise to the S and into Deng San Bu while jerking the right forearm in the same direction.

Solution: 52A, 53A, 55A. The defender blocks a punch and then swings at the opponent's head with his right arm. At this point the opponent will duck so that the defender's right arm swings past the attacker's head (fig. 54). In order to counter the duck, the defender will jerk his body back into the opponent, and hit him in the neck with the forearm.

Technique 26

Form: 56, 57 (N). Turn counterclockwise to the N and repeat 27 and 28.
Solution: 27A.

Technique 27

Form: 58 (N). Repeat 18.
Solution: 18A, 18B.

Technique 28

Form: 59, 60 (N). Repeat 19 and 31.
Solution: 19A, 31A.

55

56

57

55a

58

59

60

61

62

63

62a

63a

Technique 29

Form: 61 (N). Retract the right leg and swing the right arm down.

Solution: Mirror image of 18A and 18B.

Technique 30

Form: 62, 63 (N). Step forward with the right leg and move the right hand clockwise with the palms facing out. Step forward with the left leg into Deng San Bu and strike over the top with the left forearm into the right hand.

Solution: 62A, 63A. The defender blocks from the inside and strikes the opponent's head with his left hand.

Technique 31

Form: 64, 65 (N). Turn the left hand up so that the palm is facing out. Push the left hand forward and kick Deng Twe with the right leg while swinging the right hand back; all the fingers in the right hand are touching each other.

Solution: 65A. As the opponent punches, the defender's left hand blocks up and his right leg kicks the attacker's belly.

Technique 32

Form: 66, 67 (N). Withdraw the leg and circle counterclockwise with the left hand. Step back with the right leg into Deng San Bu while swinging the right arm over the head and into the left hand.

Solution: 66A, 67A. As the attacker punches, the defender blocks, pulls the attacker's hand, and strikes the side of his head.

Technique 33

Form: 68, 69 (N). The right hand circles clockwise while the left knee is raised. The left leg then steps back into Deng San Bu while the left arm strikes over the top into the right hand.

Solution: Same as 66A, 67A.

64

65

66

65a

66a

67

67a

68

69

95

70   71   72

70a   71a   72a

Technique 34

    Form: 70, 71 (SE). Bring both fists to your waist while raising the right knee and turning to the SE. The right leg steps forward into Deng San Bu while striking with the side of the palms.

    Solution: 70A, 71A. The defender blocks a punch to the waist by knocking the attacker's fist away. The defender then cuts the waist.

Technique 35

    Form: 72, 73 (N). Turn to N while swinging the left hand across the body. Withdraw the left hand and punch with the right.

    Solution: 72A, 73A. The defender blocks with his left hand and punches the attacker's chest.

Finish

    Form: 74, 75, 76. These forms represent the martial artist untucking his gown in order to finish the sequence. Bring both hands to the waist with the back of the hands facing each other. Move the hands up, out and then down while slightly squatting. Return to fig. 3.

73

74

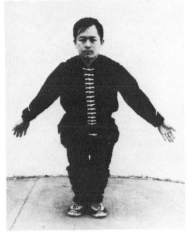

75

73a

76

77

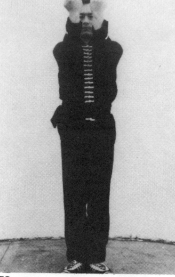

78

78a

GUNG LI CHUAN

Once the student is competent in Lien Bu Chuan he moves to Gung Li Chuan ("power training sequence") which will also train his stability and smoothness, but which, in addition, will develop his power. Every technique of the power training sequence has been especially constructed for this goal. Although Long Fist specializes in kicking, the first two sequences involve only a few kicks because a foundation in stability, smoothness, speed, and power must be developed.

Greeting

> **Form:** 77 (N). Fists at waist, toes point out at 45 degrees.

Technique 1

> **Form:** 78, 79 (N). Thrust arms up and twist them so palms face out.
>
> **Solution:** 78A, 79A, 79B, 79C. As opponent grabs the clothes, the defender's upward moving arms will break the grip. Next, in a form that is not shown in the regular sequence, the arms are locked around the opponent's neck to pull it down while the defender jumps to kick with the knee.

Technique 2

> **Form:** 80, 81 (N). Bring your fists to your ears, palms down, and switch into Ma Bu while punching down with both fists.
>
> **Solution:** 80A, 81A. As attacker strikes with a double punch to the sides of the head, the defender blocks and punches to the waist.

79

80

81

79a

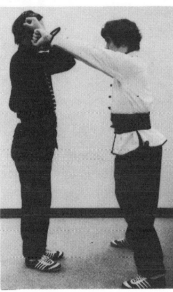

80a

81a

79b

79c

82
83
84

82a
83a
84a

Technique 3

    Form: 82 (N), 83 (W). Bring the right fist to the waist and circle counterclockwise with the left hand until the left shoulder is reached. Withdraw the left hand to the waist and punch N with the right fist. At the same time, switch to Deng San Bu so hips face W. Your face looks N.

  Solution: 82A, 83A. The left hand of the defender blocks a punch from the outside while the right hand punches.

Technique 4

    Form: 84, 85 (W). Turn head W. Swing both fists to ears and punch down.

  Solution: 84A, 85A. The attacker attempts to double punch the head. The defender blocks and punches to the waist.

Technique 5

    Form: 86 (N), 87 (E). Turn the body N and into Ma Bu while swinging the right hand across body. Keep turning until hips face E in Deng San Bu. As the body is turning, punch out with the left arm. Your head looks N.

  Solution: 86A, 87A. The solution is the mirror image of 82A and 83A. Block from the outside and punch.

100

85

86

87

85a

86a

87a

101

88

89

90

88a

89a

90a

90b

91

92

93

93a

Technique 6

> **Form:** 88, 89 (E). Turn your head E and swing fists to ears. Punch to the midsection area.
>
> **Solution:** 88A, 89A. The defender blocks the double palm attack to the temples and punches down.

Technique 7

> **Form:** 90, 91, 92 (E). Cross both hands and swing them in a circle while stepping forward with the left leg. Bring fists to the waist and bring the legs together.
>
> **Solution:** 90A, 90B. The defender blocks and kicks. (The kick is not shown in the sequence.)

Technique 8

> **Form:** 93 (N). Step the left leg N into Deng San Bu and punch straight with both fists.
>
> **Solution:** 93A. As the attacker attempts a hooking punch, the defender steps in and punches with both fists. The left fist blocks and slides forward to punch. At the same time the left fist blocks, the right fist punches low.

94

95

96

94a

95a

96a

Technique 9

> **Form:** 94 (S). The left leg comes up and the body turns clockwise to S while punching slightly up.
>
> **Solution:** 94A. As the attacker punches, the defender blocks with his left arm and punches with the right fist to temple. By leaning forward, the range of attack becomes greater.

Technique 10

> **Form:** 95 (N), 96 (W). Turn N and step down with the left leg and swing the left arm across the body. Bring the right leg forward and switch into Fu Hu Bu, facing W, while swinging right fist parallel to ground. The face looks N.
>
> **Solution:** 95A, 96A. The defender blocks from outside, grabs and pulls the arm in, and strikes the kidney.

Technique 11

> **Form:** 97 (N). Turn the body N and punch while shifting into Deng San Bu.
>
> **Solution:** 97A. As the attacker punches, the defender punches high and low.

97

98

99

97a

99a

Technique 12

Form: 98, 99 (S). Step back with the right leg into Dsao Pan Bu, fists at waist, and punch up.

Solution: 99A. As the attacker punches, the defender moves in with the crab step to punch.

100

101

102

101a

102a

Technique 13

Form: 100, 101, 102, 103 (E). Turn clockwise into E and Ma Bu while swinging the right hand across the body to position in 101. Move the left leg to the right, squatting slightly, while swinging the left hand past the right arm in a circle. As the left hand reaches right, withdraw the right hand to the waist. Stand straight and punch up.

Solution: 101A, 102A, 103A. The defender blocks the punch to the side. Then, using his left hand, the defender reaches under the attacker's arm and slides it to the left: this opens up the attacker. The defender next punches the chin.

Technique 14

Form: 104 (E), 105 (N). Swing left to the waist. Kick Deng Twe N.

Solution: 104A, 105A. The defender blocks the punch and kicks to the waist or knee.

103

104

105

103a

104a

105a

106

107

108

106a

107a

108a

Technique 15

Form: 106, 107, 108 (N). Swing the left arm up and back. Immediately follow this with the right arm swinging up and then down. At the same time, step into Deng San Bu. Next, kick Lieu Twe.

Solution: 106A, 107A, 108A. As the opponent punches, the defender blocks and strikes with an overhead smash to the eye bridge. A kick to the groin, abdomen, or face follows.

Technique 16

Form: 109 (W), 110 (N). Step down with the right leg and turn W into Ma Bu with arms in front of the face. Shift into Deng San Bu N and swing arms apart.

Solution: 109A, 110A. The defender blocks with both arms and turns hips to strike.

109

110

111

109a

110a

112

113

114

112a

113a

114a

112b

115

116

117

116a
117a

Technique 17

Form: 111, 112, 113, 114 (W). Turn W, bring arms together and shift into Gin Gi Du Li—right leg up. Move the left hand forward and the right hand back with palms down. Step back with the right leg while shifting the stance into Deng San Bu and swinging the left palm up. Shift into Ssu Lieu Bu and punch with the left fist.

Solution: 112A, 112B, 113A, 114A. When the opponent punches, the defender blocks. Next, the defender may kick to the abdomen. In the sequence, a groin attack is shown. After attacking the groin, punch the face quickly.

Technique 18

Form: 115 (W), 116 (W), 117 (W), 118 (E). Bring the left leg back and swing the arm down. Step forward with the left leg, and move the left arm across the body. Bring the right leg up and forward into Gin Gi Du Li while swinging the right arm forward. Step down in Deng San Bu facing E while swinging the right hand down. The face looks W.

Solution: 116A, 117A, 118A. The defender blocks. As the attacker's right leg comes forward, he can kick Shao Twe to knee. In the sequence, the solution which is shown has the defender blocking and striking the groin.

118

119

120

118a

121

122

123

124

125

126

126a

Technique 19
    Form: 119 (S), 120 (W). Same as 109 and 110.
  Solution: Same as 109A and 110A.

Technique 20
    Form: 121, 122, 123, 124 (S). Turn S and repeat 111, 112, 113, and 114.
  Solution: Same as 112A, 112B, 113A, and 114A.

127

128

129

127a

128a

129a

130

131

132

133   134   135

Technique 21

Form: 125, 126, 127, 128, 129 (S). Retreat, same as 115, and swing the left arm up while shifting to Deng San Bu. Swing left arm down while moving the right arm up and then in. At the same time step forward. As the right arm swings in, the left makes a big circle clockwise at the side of the body. Once the left arm is in the position of figure 128, snap the right fist forward and the left backward.

Solution: 126A, 127A, 128A, 129A. The defender blocks a punch and then attempts to strike with the right fist from overhead—but the attacker blocks it. Next, the defender hooks the attacker's blocking hand with his own striking hand and pulls it down; immediately, the left hand of the defender slides the fist away, (fig. 128A); the right hand of the defender is then free to attack (fig. 129A).

Technique 22

Form: 130, 131, 132, 133, 134 (N). Turn counterclockwise to N and repeat 115, 126, 127, 128, and 129.

Solution: Same as 126A, 127A, 128A, 129A.

136

137

138

136a

137a

138a

Technique 23

    Form: 135, 136, 137, 138, 139 (N). This technique is exactly like 21 and 22 except the feet and hands are switched.

  Solution: 136A, 137A, 138A, 139A. Same as the solutions for 21 and 22 only the roles of the hands are switched.

Technique 24

    Form: 140, 141, 142, 143, 144 (N). Same as the directions for technique 21.

  Solution: Same as the solution for technique 21.

139

140

141

139a

142

143

144

145

146

147

148

149

150

149a

151

152

153

Technique 25
Form: 145 (N). Lift the left leg and assume 94.
Solution: Same as 94A.

Technique 26
Form: 146 (S), 147 (E). Step S with left leg and repeat 95 and 96.
Solution: Same as 95A and 96A.

Technique 27
Form: 148 (S). Repeat 97.
Solution: Same as 97A.

Technique 28
Form: 149 (N). Turn 180 degrees counterclockwise and strike up while lifting the right leg.
Solution: 149A. As attacker punches, the defender blocks and counterattacks from an inside position.

Technique 29
Form: 150 (S), 151 (E). Turn S and swing the right arm across the body. Bring the left leg forward while swinging the left arm parallel to the ground, shifting into Fu Hu Bu.
Solution: Same as 95A and 96A but switch the role of the hands.

Technique 30
Form: 152 (S). Repeat 93.
Solution: Same as 93A.

Technique 31
Form: 153 (N). Repeat 94.
Solution: Same as 94A.

154

155

156

157

158

159

157a

158a

159a

160

161

162

160a

161a

162a

Technique 32
Form: 154, 155 (S). Repeat 95 and 96.
Solution: Same as 95A and 96A.

Technique 33
Form: 156 (S). Repeat 97.
Solution: Same as 97A.

Technique 34
Form: 157 (N). Turn N into Deng San Bu and block up with the left arm while swinging the right hand down and up. The left hand retreats to the shoulder.
Solution: 157A. The defender blocks the punch and attacks the opponent's groin.

Technique 35
Form: 158, 159, 160 (N). Stand Ssu Lieu Bu and punch with the left fist. Shift into Deng San Bu and push the right hand down. Stand Ssu Lieu Bu again and punch with the left fist.
Solution: 158A, 159A, 160A. The defender punches and has his fist blocked. He shifts forward and pushes down the blocking hand of the attacker. This clears the attacker's face for the punch to the face in 160A.

Technique 36
Form: 161, 162, 163 (N). Shift into Deng San Bu and swing left arm across the body. Jump forward cocking the right fist behind the ear. Land in Chi Lin Bu, right leg on toe, and punch down.
Solution: 161A, 162A, 163A. This technique is meant for defense against a rod attack. As the attacker stings, the defender blocks and jumps in to punch the belly.

163

164

165

163a

164a

165a

166

167

168

169   170   171

172   173

Technique 37
> **Form:** 164 (E), 165 (N). Spin 180 degrees counterclockwise while swinging the hand across the body and switching into Deng San Bu. Strike with the right fist from over the top while shifting to Ssu Lieu Bu.
>
> **Solution:** 164A, 165A. The defender blocks and strikes from the top.

Technique 38
> **Form:** 166 (S). Turn S and repeat 157.
>
> **Solution:** Same as 157A.

Technique 39
> **Form:** 167, 168, 169 (S). Repeat 158, 159, 114.
>
> **Solution:** Same as 158A, 159A and 114A.

Technique 40
> **Form:** 170 (S), 171 (S), 172 (S), 173 (N). Repeat 115, 116, 117, 118.
>
> **Solution:** Same as 116A, 117A, 118A.

174

175

176

174a

175a

176a

174b

176b

177

178

179

177a

178a

179a

Technique 41

Form: 174, 175, 176, 177 (S). Turn S into Deng San Bu and swing the right hand out. Lower right arm and make a circle outside to inside with the left hand. Next, punch the right fist into the left palm. Jump up and slap both hands over the knee. Step with the right leg forward into Deng San Bu and cut with the palm.

Solution: 174A, 174B, 175A, 176A, 176B, 177A. The defender blocks the punch from the outside and pulls the attacker's fist down while hooking the opponent's neck. The defender punches up, pulls the opponent into a knee kick and then attacks the waist.

Technique 42

Form: 178 (S), 179 (S), 180 (N). Turn the right palm up and then slide the left hand up while raising the right leg. Swing the left arm up, down and to the back while turning the body to face N.

Solution: 178A, 179A. As the attacker punches, the defender slides a block up and grabs the throat. The defender then turns to rip out the throat.

180

181

182

183

184

185

184a

185a

186

187

186a

Technique 43
    Form: 181 (N). Repeat 177.
  Solution: Same as 177A.

Technique 44
    Form: 182, 183 (N). Repeat 178 and 179.
  Solution: Same as 178A and 179A.

Technique 45
    Form: 184 (S). Turn 180 degrees clockwise to N while shifting to Deng San Bu and swinging the right arm up at an angle.
  Solution: 184A. As the punch is thrown the defender pushes it away and strikes the shoulder blade.

Technique 46
    Form: 185, 186 (N). Turn back 180 degrees to N while swinging the right palm down and then up. Shift into Ssu Lieu Bu while punching with the left fist. The right hand moves up.
  Solution: 185A, 186A. The defender blocks from underneath as the opponent grabs his shirt from behind. The defender then punches.

Close
    Form: 187 (N). Repeat 77 by moving the right leg up.

188   189   190

YI LU MEI FU

Yi Lu Mei Fu, which builds on Lien Bu Chuan and Gung Li Chuan, is the foundation for the advanced techniques and sequences of Long Fist; this sequence is much harder than the first two. Yi Lu Mei Fu means the "First Way of Ambush" and as the name implies, contains more tricky or subtle techniques of defense and attack than the first two sequences. The advanced techniques usually contain a simultaneous use of hands and legs. In addition, Yi Lu Mei Fu contains escape and withdrawal techniques, but at a more advanced level.

Greeting

 Form: 188 (N). The fists are at the waist.

Technique 1

 Form: 189, 190, 191 (NW). Step with the left leg to the NW and strike out with both hands while bringing the right instep behind the left knee. Step back into the original position, assuming Shuen Gi Bu while moving both arms back and down.

 Solution: 191A. Figure 189 is used as a training method for balance. With opponents on either side of the defender, he grabs their arms and pulls down. If a third opponent is in front, then the defender can kick.

191

192

193

191a

129

194

195

196

194a

195a

196a

Technique 2

   Form: 192, 193, 194, 195, 196 (N). Thrust both hands out. Move the right hand back in a semicircle, then move the left hand back in a semicircle, 194, 195. Kick Ti Twe.

   Solution: 194A, 195A, 196A. The defender blocks the punch to the side. Then, with his left hand, he opens the attacker, and kicks to the body.

Technique 3

   Form: 197, 198, 199 (N). Step forward with feet together and swing the back of the wrists to the front. Bring both hands down and in, and then out in a swinging motion.

   Solution: 197A, 198A, 199A. The opponent attacks the head and the defender blocks. Next, the defender pulls the opponent's hands down and quickly strikes his face.

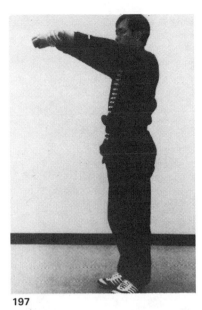

197

198

199

197a

198a

199a

131

200

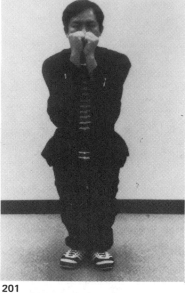

201

202

201a

202a

Technique 4

    Form: 200, 201, 202 (N). Swing the arms down, up, and in while squatting slightly. Spring up and punch to both sides.

Solution: 201A, 202A. The opponent attempts to double punch but the defender blocks and punches the face.

Technique 5

    Form: 203, 204, 205 (W). Turn both fists up and kick Lieu Twe to W. At the top of the kick quickly hook the leg down into Gin Gi Du Li stance.

Solution: 203A, 204A. The defender blocks the punch and then kicks.

203

204

205

203a

204a

206

207

208

207a

Technique 6

Form: 206, 207, 208, 209 (W). Step down with the right leg and simultaneously bring both arms together while kicking Lieu Twe. At the top of the kick, hook the leg back into Gin Gi Du Li. Slap both hands down on the left knee while hopping to switch leg position from standing on the left leg to standing on the right leg.

Solution: 207A, 209A. As the opponent punches, the defender blocks and kicks up into the opponent's belly. The defender then grabs the opponent and kicks him with the knee.

Technique 7

Form: 210, 211 (W). Hop into a low Shuen Gi Bu with a false left leg, while pushing the left hand across the body and poking the right hand slightly down.

Solution: 210A, 211A. The defender pushes the punch away and attacks the groin.

209

210

211

209a

210a

211a

212

213

214

212a

213a

214a

212b

215

216

217

215a

217a

Technique 8

Form: 212 (W). Stand up into Gin Gi Du Li while moving both hands up.

Solution: 212A, 212B. The defender uses both hands to block, or he blocks with the right hand and uses the left hand to attack the opponent's armpit. The defender follows through with a kick to the knee after the block.

Technique 9

Form: 213, 214 (W). Set the leg down and swing the left arm across the body. Punch with the right fist.

Solution: 213A, 214A. The defender blocks and punches.

Technique 10

Form: 215 (W). Kick Ti Twe with the right leg while striking forward with left palm. The toe and palm should hit each other.

Solution: 215A. The defender simultaneously strikes the face and kicks the groin of his opponent.

Technique 11

Form: 216 (W). Set the right leg back and punch. Repeat 214.

Solution: Same as 214A.

218

219

220

218a

219a

220a

Technique 12

Form: 217, 218, 219, 220 (W). Shift into Ssu Lieu Bu and move the right palm back across the body. Swing the left arm out and in while lifting the left leg up and moving the right hand across the abdomen. Swing the left arm in front and down while shifting to Shuen Gi Bu. Simultaneously, swing the right arm back and forward.

Solution: 217A, 218A, 219A, 220A. The defender blocks from outside with his right hand. The left hand then opens up the opponent. From 218A the defender can kick or punch the side of the head. The kick is not shown in the sequence.

Technique 13

Form: 221, 222, 223 (W). Move the right hand back, down to the waist, and forward.

Solution: 221A, 223A. The defender blocks the punch up and swings down to attack the chest.

221

222

223

221a

223a

224

225

226

225a

226a

Technique 14

Form: 224, 225, 226, 227 (W). Make a small hop forward and swing back the right arm, fingers touching. While the right arm is moving back, kick Ti Twe with the right leg. Immediately follow this by Nei Bie with the left leg. These two kicks should be completed in the air.

Solution: 225A, 226A, 227A. This technique is used against a rod attack. As the opponent stings, the defender blocks and hooks the rod to the side. The defender immediately jumps in and kicks the opponent's groin and side of the head.

Technique 15

Form: 228 (N). Sit low into Fu Hu Bu. The face looks W.

Solution: 228A. The defender bends low and back to avoid a kick.

Technique 16

Form: 229 (W). Shift into Deng San Bu, raise the left arm and punch with the right.

Solution: 229A. As the attacker punches, the defender blocks up and counterattacks to the chest.

227

228

229

227a

228a

229a

230

231

232

230a

231a

Technique 17

Form: 230, 231 (W). Cross the arms above the head and kick Lieu Twe with the right leg.

Solution: 230A, 231A. The defender blocks a punch up and then kicks to the groin or abdomen.

Technique 18

Form: 232 (N), 233 (N), 234 (N), 235 (E). Lower the right leg forward and assume Dsao Pan Bu while spreading the arms. Cross your arms above the head. Kick Nei Bei with left leg while swinging the left arm forward to slap the leg in the air. As the leg comes down, turn E and move the left hand down in back while shifting into Shuen Gi Bu. The face looks W.

Solution: 233A, 234A. The defender blocks a punch and attacks the opponent's head. The defender's left hand pushes the attacker's head into the kick.

233

234

235

233a

234a

236

237

238

236a

237a

238a

Technique 19

Form: 236 (S). Turn S and slap the side of the right leg with the right palm. Assume Gin Gi Du Li. The face looks W.

Solution: 236A. As the attacker kicks, the defender swings and slides the kick away while hooking it.

Technique 20

Form: 237 (S), 238 (N). Swing the right arm around while jumping and spinning 180 degrees to N. Land in a low crouch and punch down.

Solution: 237A, 238A. The defender blocks and punches to the area above the knee.

Technique 21

Form: 239, 240 (S). Step back (E) with the left leg and swing the left arm back and across the body. Bring the right leg back and assume a low crouch. At the same time swing the right hand, fingers touching, down in front of the body.

Solution: 240A. The defender blocks the punch and stoops low to hook the opponent's leg to trip him.

239

240

241

240a

241a

145

242   243   244

242a   243a

Technique 22

Form: 241, 242, 243 (W). Step W and swing the right arm across the body. Step again and swing the left arm across the body. Withdraw the left hand and punch with the right fist.

Solution: 241A, 242A, 243A. As the attacker punches, the defender blocks from the outside with his right hand. The left hand swings under the opponent's punching hand and pushes it away—opening him for attack. The defender then punches.

Technique 23

Form: 244, 245 (W). Repeat 215 and 216.

Solution: Same as 215A and 214A.

Technique 24

Form: 246, 247, 248 (W). Turn the right palm upward and slide the left hand up forming a Finger Tip Hand at the top.

Solution: 246A, 248A. The defender blocks a punch and then attacks the eyes.

245

246

247

246a

248

249

248a

250

251

250a

Technique 25
    Form: 249, 250, 251, 252 (E). Turn E and assume Fu Hu Bu. Move the right hand to the toe and then up and forward while shifting to Deng San Bu. Stand in Gin Gi Du Li.
    Solution: 250A, 252A. The defender lowers his body to pick up sand or a stone and throws it in the face of his opponent.

Technique 26
    Form: 253, 254, 255, 256, 257 (E). Walk Hsing Bu for five steps while looking W.
    Solution: 254A. The defender is walking away from an opponent who is behind and chasing him.

252

253

254

252a

254a

255

256

257

258

259

260

258a

259a

260a

Technique 27

Form: 258, 259 (W). Turn counterclockwise to W while swinging the left arm across the body. Assume Shuen Gi Bu as in 258. Immediately slap the left knee with the right palm while assuming Gin Gi Du Li.

Solution: 258A, 259A. As the opponent punches, the defender blocks. After being blocked, the attacker kicks, but the right hand of the defender blocks it.

Technique 28

Form: 260, 261, 262 (W). Step down into Ssu Lieu Bu while moving the left hand up. Jump Dan Tiao, land in Ssu Lieu Bu, right leg forward, and swing right fist down from the top.

Solution: 260A, 261A, 262A. As the attacker punches, the defender blocks and jumps in to strike the opponent in the head. This form may also be used against a rod attack.

Technique 29

Form: 263 (W). Switch into Deng San Bu, move the right hand up, and punch with the left hand.

Solution: 263A. The defender blocks the punch up and attacks the chest.

261

262

263

261a

262a

263a

264

265

266

264a

265a

Technique 30

    Form: 264 (W), 265 (W), 266 (S). Swing the left arm up and back. Simultaneously kick Deng Twe with the left leg and punch with the right fist. Retract the left leg and stand Gin Gi Du Li.

    Solution: 264A, 265A. As the attacker punches, the defender blocks with his left arm and then attacks simultaneously with a kick and punch.

Technique 31

    Form: 267, 268, 269 (S). Step down and cross the hands. Jump laterally while opening up the arms and crossing the right leg in front of the left leg. Land Ma Bu.

    Solution: An escape.

267

268

269

269a

270

271

272

270a

271a

272a

270b

273 274 275

273a 274a 275a

Technique 32

Form: 269 (S), 270 (S), 271 (W), 272 (W). Stand Ma Bu with arms spread out. Switch to Shuen Gi Bu. At the same time, put the right fist on the right knee and swing the left hand up. Change the stance into Deng San Bu while moving the left hand down in front of the body. Move the left hand until it is below the right hand. Quickly slap the right hand forward.

Solution: 269A, 270A, 271A, 272A. As the opponent punches, the defender blocks, and then hooks the punch down by going over the top of the attacker's arm. At this point a second solution is to kick the attacker's instep. After the punch has been hooked, the left hand of the defender covers the punch, thus allowing the right hand to attack.

Technique 33

Form: 273, 274 (W). Form an Eagle Claw and punch with the left fist.

Solution: 273A, 274A. The defender blocks, grabs, and punches.

Technique 34

Form: 275 (W). Punch with the right fist while kicking Deng Twe with the left leg.

Solution: 275A. As the opponent punches, the defender deflects the attack and kicks and punches at the same time.

155

276

277

278

276a

277a

Technique 35

  Form: 276 (W). Step down and repeat Technique 34, but switch the hands and legs.

  Solution: 276A. Same as 275A except from a different side.

Technique 36

  Form: 277, 278 (W). Repeat 275 and 276 in the air while jumping. Land in Ssu Lieu Bu while punching a third time.

  Solution: 277A. Same as 275A and 276A, only the attack also includes a jump.

Technique 37

  Form: 279 (W), 280 (W), 281 (N), 282 (E), 283 (E). Hop forward off the back leg and land in Ssu Lieu Bu, arm extended. Swing the right arm across the body and then to the lower chest. When the right arm reaches the chest, assume Dsao Pan Bu and swing the left arm across the body. Kick Chao Twe with the left leg while swinging the left arm W; the momentum of the kick should swing the body so it faces E as in 282. Bring the right leg in to assume Gin Gi Du Li.

  Solution: 280A, 281A, 282A. As the opponent punches, the defender blocks and turns his body while cocking his left arm. The defender then kicks the attacker's leg while pushing across the neck with the left hand. The last form is for anticipating an opponent.

156

279

280

281

280a

281a

282

283

284

282a

285

286

287

Technique 38

    Form: 284, 285, 286, 287 (E). Walk five steps in Hsing Bu.
  Solution: Same as 254A.

Technique 39

    Form: 288, 289 (W). Repeat 258 and 259.
  Solution: Same as 258A and 259A.

Technique 40

    Form: 290, 291, 292 (W). Step with the left leg forward, jump Dan Tiao while block-
        ing with the left arm, and kick Chei Twe. Assume Dsao Pan Bu and punch
        with the right fist.

288

289

290

291

292

293

291a

292a

293a

Solution: 291A, 292A. This technique is used against a rod attack. As the opponent attacks, the defender pushes away the rod and kicks the knee. The defender then moves in and punches the attacker's waist.

294

295

296

294a

295a

296a

Technique 41
Form: 293, 294, 295 (W). Move the right palm up. Step forward into Ssu Lieu Bu while swinging the left palm up. Punch with the right fist.
Solution: 293A, 294A, 295A. As the opponent attacks with a rod, the defender pushes it up and steps in, once again pushing the rod up. The defender then punches.

Technique 42
Form: 296, 297 (E). Turn counterclockwise to E while swinging the left arm across the body. Assume Ssu Lieu Bu and punch with the right fist.
Solution: 296A, 297A. The defender blocks and punches.

Technique 43
Form: 298, 299 (E). Kick Shain Fon Twe with the right leg. Land in Ssu Lieu Bu and punch with the right fist.
Solution: 298A. The defender attacks.

Technique 44
Form: 300, 301, 302 (E). Turn the right palm up. Step forward while sliding the left palm up along the right arm and assuming Gin Gi Du Li. Hook the left hand down.
Solution: This solution is the same as 246A and 248A. Only the right leg is held up.

297

298

299

297a

298a

300

301

302

YI LU MEI FU

303

304

305

Technique 45

Form: 303, 304, 305 (W). Repeat 249, 250, 251.

Solution: Same as 250A.

Technique 46

Form: 306 (W). Swing the right arm up and back, while striking forward with the left palm. While the hands are moving, stand Gin Gi Du Li.

Solution: 306A, 306B. As the opponent punches, the defender blocks the fist up and strikes the chest. The second solution is to kick.

Technique 47

Form: 307, 308 (W). Swing the right hand across the body while moving the left hand across the waist. Hop into Shuen Gi Bu, left leg forward, while punching up with the left fist.

Solution: 307A, 307B, 308A. The right hand blocks the attacker's punch away. The defender then may kick the attacker's knee. After blocking, the left fist swings up into the opponent.

Close

Form: 309 (W), 310 (W), 311 (W), 312 (E), 313 (N), 314 (N). Step back with the left leg and bring hands down. Swing both arms up and forward, down, and back while stepping back with the right leg into Deng San Bu. Swing both arms down, up, and forward. Turn 180 degrees clockwise to E while changing stance to Deng San Bu. Bring feet together, make a fist with the right hand, turn the fist palm down, and squat. Next, stand up. This action represents the untucking of the gown. Refer to Lien Bu Chuan for the opening and closing forms.

306

307

308

306a

307a

308a

306b

307b

309

310

311

312

313

314

CHAPTER 4
MIDDLE LEVEL
SEQUENCES

Once the sequences in the third chapter can be done smoothly and with stability, the student will move on to the middle level sequences. In this volume only two middle level sequences will be shown, although there are more. The techniques in the middle level sequences are more difficult and will thus require a solid foundation in the fundamental sequences. If the student masters these middle level sequences, then he will have to seek out a qualified Long Fist master to learn the remaining middle and advanced sequences.

SHAW FU IEN

The purpose of this middle level sequence is to teach the Long Fist student the principles, ideas, and techniques of Northern Praying Mantis, which have been modified to fit the stylistic features of Long Fist.

SHAW FU IEN

1

2

3

4

5

6

5a

6a

Greeting

   Form: 1 (N). Fists at waist

7   8   9

8a

Technique 1

    Form: 2, 3, 4 (N). Step with the left leg into Deng San Bu and thrust out both arms. Step back into Shuen Gi Bu and kick Ti Twe with the left leg.

  Solution: The same as the opening technique of Yi Lu Mei Fu.

Technique 2

    Form: 5 (N), 6 (W). Step forward, feet together, and make circles with both arms in front of the body. The right arm moves clockwise and the left counterclockwise. Turn W and thrust the right arm down while shifting to Deng San Bu.

  Solution: 5A, 6A. The defender blocks and attacks the groin.

Technique 3

    Form: 7, 8 (W). Hook down with the right hand. Pull the right hand to the armpit while striking out with the back of the wrist as in 8.

  Solution: 8A. As the opponent punches, the defender slides the punch away and strikes simultaneously.

Technique 4

    Form: 9, 10 (W). Bring the left leg back and step forward again while swinging the left hand across body. Step forward with the right leg into Deng San Bu and punch with the right fist.

  Solution: 10A. The defender blocks and punches.

10

11

12

10a

12a

13

14

15

14a

16   17   18

16a   17a   18a

Technique 5

    Form: 11, 12 (E). Turn 180 degrees counterclockwise to E while swinging the left hand across the body and striking with the right fist. The stance is Deng San Bu.

    Solution: 12A. Block, and strike the head.

Technique 6

    Form: 13, 14 (W). Turn 180 degrees clockwise to W while swinging the right hand across the body and striking with the left fist. The stance is Deng San Bu.

    Solution: 14A. Same as 12A but with different hands.

Technique 7

    Form: 15 (W), 16 (S). Make a counterclockwise circle with the left hand while bringing the feet together. Stamp the right foot and punch down with the right fist.

    Solution: 16A. As the opponent punches, the defender blocks and punches above the knee.

Technique 8

    Form: 17, 18 (W). Jump up and turn the hips 180 degrees clockwise while swinging both arms across the body. After landing, shift into Deng San Bu and punch with the right fist.

    Solution: 17A, 18A. As the opponent punches, the defender jumps to knock away the punch. When the defender lands, he attacks.

19

20

21

19a

20a

21a

Technique 9

Form: 19 (W). Kick Ti Twe with the right leg while striking forward with the left palm. The palm hits the toe.

Solution: 19A. Simultaneous attack to the groin and face.

Technique 10

Form: 20 (W). Raise the right fist to the ear and punch down while slapping the fist to the left palm. The stance is Ssu Lieu Bu.

Solution: 20A. The defender blocks and punches low.

Technique 11

Form: 21 (W). Kick Shain Fon Twe.

Solution: 21A. The defender attacks the opponent.

Technique 12

Form: 22 (W). Land and repeat 20.

Solution: Same as 20A.

Technique 13

Form: 23, 24 (W). Repeat 17 and 18.

Solution: Same as 17A and 18A.

22   23   24

25   26   27

Technique 14

    Form: 25, 26 (W). Punch with the left fist, then with the right fist.

Solution: Continuation of the attack in 18A.

28

29

30

28a

29a

30a

Technique 15

Form: 27, 28 (E). Swing the body 180 degrees clockwise to E while changing stance to Gin Gi Du Li and moving the right hand across body. Withdraw the right hand and swing the left fist across the body.

Solution: 28A. Defender blocks a punch and then attacks the elbow.

Technique 16

Form: 29 (E). Lift the left fist and punch with the right fist while stepping down into Ssu Lieu Bu.

Solution: 29A. The defender blocks the punch up and strikes the chest.

Technique 17

Form: 30, 31, 32 (E). Raise the right palm and right knee up while hopping forward off the back leg. Land in Ssu Lieu Bu, right leg forward, while moving the left palm up. Raise the left fist and punch with the right hand.

Solution: 30A, 31A, 32A. As the attacker punches, the defender pushes the fist up while moving forward. The left hand then pushes the opponent's arm up to free the right fist for an attack to the chest.

Technique 18

Form: 33, 34 (E). Repeat 17 and 18.

Solution: Same as 17A and 18A.

31

32

33

31a

32a

34

35

36

35a

36a

Technique 19

Form: 35 (S). Swing the right palm down to the right leg while shifting into Fu Hu Bu.

Solution: 35A. The defender quickly strikes the attacker's leg while the punch is in progress.

Technique 20

Form: 36 (E), 37 (N), 38 (N). Turn E into Deng San Bu and swing the right wrist into the left palm. Turn counterclockwise to N while assuming Ma Bu and making a clockwise circle. Once the circling hand is at the waist, thrust it forward.

Solution: 36A, 38A. The defender blocks a punch, uses the left hand to keep the opponent's arm stable, and then attacks the groin.

Technique 21

Form: 39, 40 (E). Turn E while swinging the right arm up and shifting to Deng San Bu. Slide the left hand behind the right arm and jump into Tun Bu while thrusting out the left arm. The left leg is forward.

Solution: 39A, 40A. As the opponent punches, the defender blocks, slides his left hand under the attacker's hand and shifts his stance to Tun Bu. The defender may punch with the right hand.

37

38

39

38a

39a

40

41

42

40a

Technique 22

Form: 41, 42, 43, 44, 45 (E). Hop forward and assume the stance in 40, but a bit higher. Jump forward off the right leg and punch with the right fist. Immediately bring the left hand in front of the right fist as the right arm is bent inward. Swing the right hand up so that it slaps out. Next, swing the right hand in, down, out, and under the left hand, with fingers touching and pointing down. This whole hand motion must be done while in the air. Land in Gin Gi Du Li as in 45.

Solution: 43A, 44A, 44B, 45A. The hand technique is a combination which can be used if an opponent blocks one or two punches. As the defender punches, the opponent blocks. Next, the left hand takes away the blocking hand to allow a strike up, but this is also blocked. The left hand then slides up to push away the blocking hand while the right hand swings underneath to strike the chin.

176

43

44

45

43a

44a

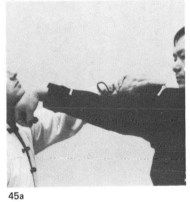

45a

44b

46

47

48

49

50

Technique 23

Form: 46 (N), 47 (N), 48 (W). Step with the left leg down and assume Fu Hu Bu. Swing the left hand to the toe and raise the body up to Deng San Bu while punching with the right fist.

Solution: Sweeping the hand past the leg will block a low kick. Once the kick is blocked, a punch is thrown.

Technique 24

Form: 49 (W). Repeat 19.
Solution: Same as 19A.

Technique 25

Form: 50, 51, 52, 53, 54 (W). Step with the right leg down into Shuen Gi Bu while swinging both arms down, out, and up so palms face out. Shift into Deng San Bu and bring the left hand down while moving the right hand down and across body. When the right hand reaches the waist, thrust up with the left hand. Hook the left hand down and swing it down so that it slaps the side of the left leg. While doing the above, jump off the right leg and kick Ti Twe while thrusting out the right palm; the right palm and toe should hit each other.

Solution: 52A, 52B, 53A, 54A. As the opponent attempts to punch low, the defender blocks down and thrusts his fingers into the opponent's neck. But the opponent blocks the finger thrust. Next, the defender hooks the opponent's left hand down and simultaneously strikes his face and groin.

51

52

53

52a

53a

52b

54

55

54a

56

55a

56a

57

58

59

57a

58a

59a

Technique 26

    Form: 55 (N). Jump up and kick Ba Bu Gan Chan with the left leg. The face looks W.

    Solution: 55A. As the opponent punches, the defender attacks the instep.

Technique 27

    Form: 56 (S). Keep low and turn the body clockwise while kicking Shao Tan Twe. The face looks W.

    Solution: 56A. As the opponent punches, the defender kicks his leg out.

Technique 28

    Form: 57 (W). Turn 90 degrees to W while swinging the left arm across the body and kicking Shao Twe.

    Solution: 57A. The defender blocks a punch and then kicks the opponent's knee.

Technique 29

    Form: 58 (N). Step down and strike W with left elbow while squatting low. The right leg is on its toes and its knee is pointing E.

    Solution: 58A. An elbow strike to the opponent's chest.

Technique 30

    Form: 59 (E). Thrust the right hand E.

    Solution: 59A. The defender attacks the opponent's groin.

60

61

62

61a

63

64

65

66

67

68

66a

67a

Technique 31

    Form: 60, 61 (E). Hook the right hand down. Slide the right hand to the right armpit and thrust out the left hand, all the fingers touching, while shifting into Tun Bu.

    Solution: 61A. As the opponent attempts to punch, the defender slides the punch away and strikes to the face.

Technique 32

    Form: 62 (E), 63 (E), 64 (N), 65 (N). Retract the left leg. Swing the left arm across the body while hopping forward. Next, keep swinging the left hand until facing N while shifting into Ma Bu. Punch with the right fist.

    Solution: This is a simple block and punch.

Technique 33

    Form: 66 (N). Raise the left fist and swing the right fist down.

    Solution: 66A. The defender blocks up and then strikes the opponent's waist.

Technique 34

    Form: 67 (W). Shift to Deng San Bu facing W while swinging the right fist up into the left hand.

    Solution: 67A. The defender attacks the side of the opponent's head; then the defender left hooks the head to keep the opponent from escaping.

Technique 35

    Form: 68 (E). Turn to E while shifting into Deng San Bu and swinging the right fist down.

    Solution: Same as 66A.

69

70

71

69a

70a

71a

Solution: 69A, 70A, 71A, 72A. As the opponent punches low, the defender blocks and then locks the punching hand. Next, the defender slides his right hand over and to the outside; this is a Chin Na technique which will control the opponent's wrist. Once the opponent is controlled, the defender kicks the groin and chest.

Technique 37
Form: 73 (NW). Turn the body to NW and kick Teng Twe.
Solution: 73A. The defender kicks while the opponent punches.

Technique 36
Form: 69, 70, 71, 72 (E). Put the left hand on your right wrist. Swing both arms up and then down while making a slight jump into Tun Bu, left leg forward. Next, kick Tiao Teng Twe: kick the right leg Ti Twe and the left leg Teng Twe.

72

73

74

72a

73a

75

76

77

75a

78

79

80

81   82

Technique 38

>**Form:**   74, 75 (W). Turn W and swing the left arm across the body while punching with the right fist. The stance is Deng San Bu.

Solution: 75A. The defender blocks and punches.

Technique 39

>**Form:**   76, 77, 78, 79 (N). Turn the body N and swing back the right hand. Move the left leg so it points N and then repeat Technique 12 of Yi Lu Mei Fu.

Solution: Same as 217A, 218A and 219A of Yi Lu Mei Fu.

Close

>**Form:**   80, 81, 82 (N). Cross the left leg behind the right leg while bringing both arms in to the waist and then out with palms up. Step back with the right leg in a NE dircction so the stance is Deng San Bu, while at the same time swinging arms down. Bring the left leg to the right leg while moving the arms up in front of the face and then down. The palms face the floor once they are in front of the body and moving down.

83

84

85

86

87

88

SHIH TZU TAN

Shih Tzu Tan is a middle level sequence which builds on Yi Lu Mei Fu by adding a number of different techniques. In particular, a number of different kicks, side door attacks, and forcing techniques are added.

Greeting
Form: 83 (N). Fists at waist.

Techinque 1–4
Form: 84 to 95. Repeat the first four techniques of Yi Lu Mei Fu.
Solution: Same as those in Yi Lu Mei Fu.

89

90

91

92

93

94

95
96
97

96a

97a

Technique 5

    Form: 96 (E). Move left leg back so the stance is Deng San Bu. At the same time, turn the right forearm in.

    Solution: 96A. The right forearm blocks a punch.

Technique 6

    Form: 97, 98, 99 (E). Swing the right arm up. Move right hand to waist while the left hand swings in front of the body. Simultaneous with the hand movements, bring the right leg back so the stance is Chi Lin Bu. Bring the left hand below the right hand. Next, punch up with the right fist.

    Solution: 97A, 98A, 99A. The defender blocks the punch, pushes the punching hand down, and then attacks the opponent.

98

99

100

98a

99a

101

102

103

101a

102a

Technique 7

　Form: 100, 101, 102 (E). Bring the right leg forward so the stance is Ssu Lieu Bu while bringing both fists together. Swing both fists down and back. Punch forward with the right fist up and the left fist up and then down.

　Solution: 101A. The defender blocks down and then attacks simultaneously with both fists.

Technique 8

　Form: 103, 104 (W). Turn the body 180 degrees counterclockwise to W: the stance is still Ssu Lieu Bu. While turning, swing the right palm down and up. Bring the right hand up above the head and punch with the left fist.

　Solution: 104A. The defender blocks and punches.

Technique 9

　Form: 105, 106, 107 (N). Bend into Fu Hu Bu while bringing both fists together: the face looks W. Jump W while both hands circle as a unit counterclockwise. Make two circles with the hands; one before jumping and one during jumping.

　Solution: 105A. The defender blocks the punch down and then will jump into the opponent if he retreats.

104

105

106

104a

105a

107

108

109

110

111

112

110a

111a

112a

194

113

114

115

114a

Technique 10

Form: 108, 109 (W). Land in Ssu Lieu Bu, left leg forward, and repeat the hand motions of 101 and 102, except reversing the hands.

Solution: Same as 101A and 102A.

Technique 11

Form: 110 (N). Shift into Ma Bu while turning N. At the same time, swing the left fist across the body and turn the right fist up.

Solution: 110A. The defender blocks the punch up and then attacks the kidney.

Technique 12

Form: 111 (S). Jump up and turn 180 degrees counterclockwise while swinging the left arm up and right fist horizontally. Land in Ma Bu.

Solution: 111A. Same as 110A except from the opposite side.

Technique 13

Form: 112 (W). Swing both arms down and then strike with the right fist up; left fist up and then down. The hand movements are made at the same time as a shift into Deng San Bu.

Solution: 112A. The defender blocks the opponent and then attacks with both fists. The left hand can grab the head to keep the opponent from escaping.

Technique 14

Form: 113, 114 (W). Shift to Shuen Gi Bu, right leg up, while withdrawing the right fist and swinging the left fist down. Bring the left fist under the right hand. Next, punch with the right fist up.

Solution: 114A. As the opponent punches, the defender blocks and punches up.

116

117

118

116a

117a

119

120

121

122

123

124

123a   124a

Technique 15

Form: 115, 116 (W). Step back with the right leg into Shuen Gi Bu, left leg forward, and swing the right hand down until it is below the left hand. Next, punch up with the left fist.

Solution: 116A. The defender blocks down and punches up.

Technique 16

Form: 117, 118 (W). Shift into Shuen Gi Bu that is much lower and put the left fist on the knee. Raise the right fist up.

Solution: 118A. The defender blocks down and gets ready to attack.

Technique 17

Form: 119, 120, 121, 122 (W). Hop forward and again assume the same stance but higher. Kick Ti Twe with the right leg while swinging the right hand down and up so it slaps the kicking foot at its highest point. Step down into Deng San Bu and swing the right fist down.

Solution: This technique is used to train a person in withdrawing a knife from his boots. In ancient China many martial artists travelled with knives hidden in their boots. When attacked, they had to quickly take them out. In the technique, as the martial artist kicks, he slaps his hand against the foot, taking out his knife. As the right fist swings down, he stabs.

Technique 18

Form: 123 (E). Jump back while turning 180 degrees to face E while slapping out with the left hand. The right leg is raised.

Solution: 123A. The defender jumps and slaps the opponent at the side of his head.

Technique 19

Form: 124 (E). Turn 360 degrees clockwise into Deng San Bu, right leg forward, while swinging fists around.

Solution: 124A. The defender grabs the neck and strikes.

197

125

126

127

125a

126a

128

129

130

131

132

133

131a

132a

133a

Technique 20

Form: 125 (W), 126 (E), 127 (E), 128 (E). Turn 180 degrees counterclockwise into Deng San Bu while swinging the left arm across the body. Lift the right leg up into Gin Gi Du Li. Turn 180 degrees counterclockwise while shifting into Deng San Bu. At the same time, swing the right fist all the way around. Slide the left hand forward while walking Hsing Bu backwards for two steps. Next, assume 128.

Solution: 125A, 126A. As the opponent punches, the defender blocks, grabs his arm, and swings the fist into the head.

Technique 21

Form: 129, 130, 131 (E). Walk three steps in Hsing Bu and swing the right fist into the left palm.

Solution: 131A. The defender attacks the head. The left hand can be used to hold the head.

134

135

134a

136

Technique 22

> **Form:** 132, 133, 134, 135, 136 (W). Turn 180 degrees clockwise into Deng San Bu while swinging the right arm across the body. Bring the right hand to the waist and swing the left arm up and then down. Once the left hand has reached the waist, swing the right arm back, up, and then down. Keep moving the right hand down until it slaps the right toe; as this is happening the stance changes to Fu Hu Bu. Stand straight up in Gin Gi Du Li as shown in 136.

> **Solution:** 132A, 133A, 134A. The defender blocks a punch, pushes the attacker's arm down, and attacks the face.

Technique 23

> **Form:** 137, 138, 139, 140, 141, 142, 143 (W). Walk four steps in Hsing Bu. Slap the right hand against the right leg and kick Tiao Ti Twe with the right leg first. After landing, bring the right leg in front so the stance is Dsao Pan Bu and punch down with both fists.

137

138

139

140

141

142

143

144

145

143a

144a

145a

Solution: 143A. These forms are used to chase an opponent. Kick at him, and then punch.

Technique 24

Form: 144, 145 (W). Spin 360 degrees clockwise into Ssu Lieu Bu while swinging up the left hand. Punch with the right fist and raise the left hand.

Solution: 144A, 145A. The defender blocks up and punches.

Technique 25

Form: 146, 147 (E). Turn 180 degrees counterclockwise while swinging the right hand down and up, and switching into Ssu Lieu Bu, left leg forward. Punch with the left fist.

Solution: 146A, 147A. The defender blocks up and attacks the opponent's chest.

146

147

148

146a

147a

149

150

151

149a

Technique 26

Form: 148 (W), 149 (S), 150 (S). Shift to Deng San Bu, hips pointed W and face looking S, while moving the right hand against chest. Kick Lieu Twe to the S while swinging the right hand up and back and slapping the kicking leg with the left palm. Lower the kicking leg into Shuen Gi Bu as in 150.

Solution: 149A. As an attacker punches, the martial artist blocks and then kicks. The left hand is used to distract the opponent's attention from the kick.

Technique 27

Form: 151, 152, 153 (E). Stand up, move the left leg into Gin Gi Du Li and turn E. Step down and swing the left arm across the body. Jump up and kick Ba Bu Gan Chan with the right leg. Land in Fu Hu Bu and thrust out the right hand.

Solution: 152A, 153A. The defender uses a long range jump to attack the opponent's leg. Once near the opponent, the defender attacks the groin.

Technique 28

Form: 154, 155, 156 (E). Shift into Deng San Bu and swing right arm across body. Jump and kick Ba Bu Gan Chan with the left leg. Land in Fu Hu Bu and thrust out the left hand.

Solution: Same as previous technique.

152

153

154

152a

153a

155

156

157

158

159

160

159a

160a

Technique 29

    Form: 157, 158 (E). Stand in Deng San Bu, left leg forward, and swing the left arm across body. Punch with the right fist.

  Solution: The defender blocks and punches.

Technique 30

    Form: 159, 160 (E). Thrust out the left palm. At the same time, kick Ti Twe with the right leg. Retract the leg and punch with the right fist.

  Solution: 159A, 160A. As the attacker punches, the defender simultaneously kicks and punches. After kicking, the defender punches.

Technique 31

    Form: 161 (E). Shift in to Ssu Lieu Bu and raise the right fist while punching with the left hand.

  Solution: The defender blocks up and punches.

Technique 32

    Form: 162, 163, 164 (S). Repeat Technique 26.

  Solution: Same as for Technique 26.

Technique 33

    Form: 165, 166, 167 (E). Repeat Technique 27.

  Solution: Same as for Technique 27.

161

162

163

164

165

166

167

168

169

170

171

172

170a

171a

173   174   175

Technique 34

    Form: 168, 169 (E). Shift into Deng San Bu and swing the right hand across the body. Hook the left hand forward and punch up into it with the right fist.

    Solution: The defender blocks a punch, hooks the opponent's neck and punches him in the chin. Similar to Technique 41 of Gung Li Chuan.

Technique 35

    Form: 170 (E). Jump up and simultaneously kick Ti Twe with the right leg while thrusting forward with the right palm. The hand and toe should hit each other.

    Solution: 170A. The defender attacks with hands and legs together.

Technique 36

    Form: 171 (E), 172 (N). Land in Gin Gi Du Li and slap the right knee with the right hand. Turn the body clockwise N and slap the left hand against the knee while the knee is being raised.

    Solution: 171A. Both of these forms are block and hook kicks.

Technique 37

    Form: 173 (W). Step with the left leg W and into Deng San Bu while raising the left hand and punching with the right.

    Solution: The defender blocks up and punches.

Technique 38

    Form: 174, 175 (W). Raise the left leg and slap its knee with the left hand. Step down and raise the right leg while slapping its knee with the right palm.

    Solution: Both forms are block kicks.

176

177

178

177a

Technique 39
   Form: 176, 177 (W). Raise both fists to the head. Punch down with both arms while jumping into Shuen Gi Bu, left leg forward.
   Solution: 177A. As the attacker double punches, defender blocks up and then punches down.

Technique 40
   Form: 178, 179 (W). Swing the right hand up and left hand down. Punch up with the left fist.
   Solution: 179A. The defender blocks and punches.

Close
   Form: 180, 181, 182, 183, 184, 185. Repeat the ending of Yi Lu Mei Fu.

179

180

181

179a

182

183

184

SHIH TZU TAN

185

CHAPTER 5
FREE FIGHTING
STRATEGIES

The previous chapters have presented the basic elements that are needed as a foundation for effective free fighting. This chapter will show how to free fight at an elementary and middle level in order to give the martial artist a more complete perspective on Long Fist. To do this, fighting forms, techniques, and strategies will be presented. While this chapter will not present a complete discussion of Long Fist free fighting, it does lay a foundation for further research by the martial artist.

FIGHTING FORMS

Through thousands of years of research it has been found that the best way to train mental reaction, speed, and power is through the "fighting form" (*Twe Shih*). A fighting form, in review, is a continuous flowing repetition of a few techniques done by two or more students. By continuous repetition, the student develops speed, accuracy, mental reaction, and proper form. The techniques in the fighting forms are practical forms that are used in free fighting. It is obvious that fighting forms are the basis of effective free fighting because they lay the foundation for attack and defense.

The fighting forms in this chapter are only a few of the many that exist. The ones presented in this section are those typically practiced by the Long Fist stylist. After developing a solid foundation, the martial artist can construct his own fighting forms by taking any technique out of any sequence and adapting it so that the form can be smoothly practiced. In this way, there are a limitless number of fighting forms. By constant research, the martial artist can develop many effective and practical fighting forms.

The next stage after mastery of the fighting forms is to construct them in such a manner that moving forms such as dodging, escaping, forcing, etc., are also included. When two practitioners engage in a continuous number of fighting forms, the drill is called a fighting sequence. As was mentioned in Chapter 1, proficiency in fighting sequences is necessary before engaging in free sparring. The practitioners can construct their own fighting sequence from the stable ones. Once the fighting sequences have been mastered, the student is ready to go to the general strategies of free fighting, an aspect to be treated in this chapter.

When practicing any fighting form, keep in mind a few practical things. First, never let the fighting form degenerate into a mere thoughtless routine. Always concentrate when practicing a fighting form. Second, as the student improves, the speed and power of the fighting form should increase. By constantly pushing oneself to improve, the martial artist will increase his overall proficiency. Third, each fighting form must be done vigorously and continuously. And fourth, for every attack use Deng San Bu as the stance, and for every defensive maneuver use Ssu Lieu Bu. By constantly shifting forward and backward, the students train good habits of offense and defense.

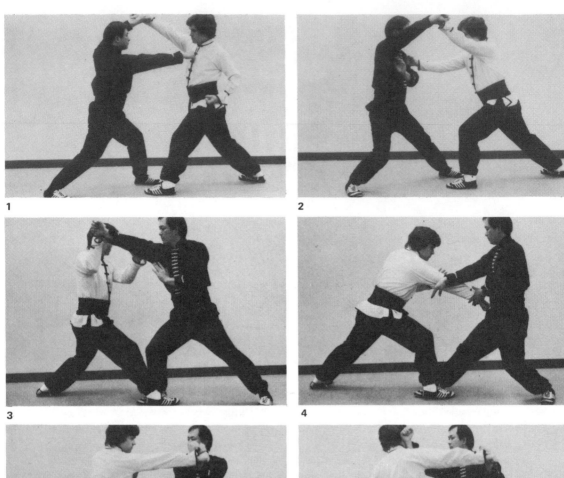

1

2

3

4

5

6

Fighting Form 1:

Figure 1: W punches B with the right fist. W's punch slides away, over B's inside block with the left hand. B then counterattacks to the chest.

Figure 2: W sits back and uses the left hand to push away B's punch. W then counterattacks to B's chest, repeating the previous form.

Fighting Form 2:

Figure 3: B uses the back of the right fist to strike up. W blocks with his right hand against W's fist while the left hand pushes the elbow.

Figure 4: W pushes away the elbow and punches down. B blocks by pushing his left hand against W's fist and by sliding his right hand to W's elbow. After blocking, B slides his right fist up to strike W. W blocks as in the previous form to begin the cycle again.

Fighting Form 3:

Figure 5: W punches and B blocks with both arms together.

7   8   9   10   11   12

Figure 6:   B's next move is to slide in and strike W's head.

Figure 7:   As B attacks the head, W slides his punching arm back to block.

Figure 8:   W slides his right fist forward to strike B's head. B blocks as in figure 5 to begin the cycle again.

Fighting Form 4:

Figure 9:   W double punches from the outside. B moves his hands to an inside position in order to block.

Figure 10:   B punches both fists down. B slides both hands over W's wrist to push away the low double punch.

Figure 11:   W uppercuts B with both fists. B slides both hands under W's fist to push away W's attack.

Figure 12:   B attacks W's temples with both fists. W slides his hands under B's fist in order to block. W then attacks B's temples. B then blocks as in figure 9 to begin the cycle again.

215

13

14

15

16

17

18

Fighting Form 5:

Figure 13: B punches with the right fist. W blocks from an inside position with the right hand.

Figure 14: B punches with the left fist. B moves his right hand across to block W's punch.

Figure 15: B punches to W's waist with the right fist. W slides his left hand down to block.

Figure 16: W punches with the right fist. B blocks with the right hand.

Figure 17: W punches with the left fist. B moves his right hand across to block.

Figure 18: W punches to B's waist with his right fist. B blocks down with the left hand. B punches with the right fist as in figure 13 to begin the cycle again.

19

20

21

22

23

24

Fighting Form 6:

Figure 19: Both practitioners stand with opposite legs forward. W hook punches to B's head with the left fist. B slides his right hand to the outside to guide away the attack.

Figure 20: B places his left hand under his own right hand. B then grabs and pulls W's arm with the left hand while retracting the right fist.

Figure 21: B attacks W's head with a hook punch.

Figure 22: W slides away his left arm and moves it to the outside in order to guide B's punch away.

Figure 23: W places his right hand under his blocking hand and then grabs and pulls B's arm while bringing back the left fist.

Figure 24: W hook punches B's head. B blocks as in figure 19 to begin the cycle again.

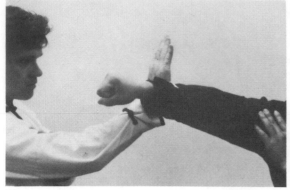

25

26

27

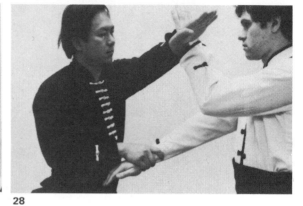

28

Fighting Form 7:

Figure 25: B punches and W blocks from the outside.

Figure 26: B grabs and pulls W's blocking hand.

Figure 27: B cuts at W's neck while holding W's hand.

Figure 28: W blocks from the outside position.

Figure 29: B grabs and pulls W's second blocking hand down, thus trapping both of W's arms.

Figure 30: B releases his bottom hand and cuts at W's neck.

Figure 31: W must quickly move his first trapped hand to block B's third attack. Continue to do this basic motion of attacking, blocking, grabbing, and trapping. Either side may at any moment take the lead. Thus, after blocking, W may pull B's hand down to begin an effort to trap B's hands.

218

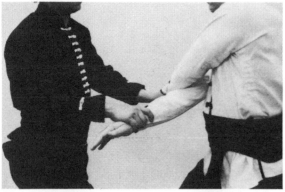

29

30

31

32

33

34

35

Fighting Form 8:

Figure 32: W punches with the right fist while B blocks with the right hand from the outside. At the same time, B twists his legs, right leg forward.

Figure 33: B steps forward with the left leg kicking Chao Twe while the left arm swings around into W's neck. B grabs and pulls W's punching hand in the process.

Figure 34: To counter B's move, W blocks B's left fist with his left hand while lifting the right leg to avoid the kick.

Figure 35: B sets his left leg down while W retreats with his right leg. B keeps his hold on W.

Figure 36: B steps forward with the right leg kicking Chao Twe while the right arm swings into W's neck.

Figure 37: W blocks with his free hand and lifts up the left leg.

Figure 38: B sets his right leg down and starts to repeat figure 33 to begin the cycle again. Later B and W switch sides.

220

36

37

38

39

40

41

42

Fighting Form 9:

Figure 39: W kicks Ti Twe at B. B attempts to hook W's leg. W must quickly retract his kick to avoid being hooked.

Figure 40: W retracts his leg and B kicks Ti Twe at W. W attempts to hook B's kicking leg. Keep alternating.

Fighting Form 10:

Figure 41: B kicks Chai Twe at W's knee.

Figure 42: B retracts his leg and W kicks Chai Twe at B's knee. Keep alternating.

Fighting Form 11:

Figure 43: W kicks Ti Twe and B attempts to hook W's leg. W must not let B hook the leg by retracting the kick as quickly as possible.

Figure 44: If B hooks W's leg, then B quickly brings up the back leg and hooks the left arm around the leg as shown in the figure. If the leg is properly locked, then B can exert pressure to cause pain and immobilize W. One side can keep kicking and the other side blocking and hooking.

Fighting Form 12:

Figure 45: W sweeps with Shao Tan Twe using the right leg. B jumps up and kicks Nei Bie.

Figure 46: W stands up and kicks Nei Bie. B ducks to avoid the kick. W sweeps again and B jumps up to kick Nei Bie. Keep doing this continuously.

Fighting Form 13:

Figure 47: Both practitioners stand facing each other. Next, both jump off the right leg at 45 degrees to the left side. While in the air, both kick toward the center with their right leg.

43

44   45   46

47   48

Fighting Form 14:

Figure 48: Both martial artists stand facing each other, right leg forward. Both sides jump up and spin 90 degrees counterclockwise. When both are in the air, they kick and thrust out their right leg and hand so that hand and leg slap each other. They keep circling around each other with continuous 90 degree counterclockwise turns.

FREE FIGHTING STRATEGIES

To begin understanding the general fighting strategies of Long Fist, it is important to know the key words of this style. Key words represent the basic characteristics and traits that a style will specialize in. In other words, key words can be said to describe the unique personality of the style. Every Wu Su division will have its own set of key words. Many times the key words are passed on to the student by means of poetry. In Long Fist there are twelve main and five subsidiary key words. The major key words are "Raise" (*Ti*), "Catch" (*Na*), "Seal" (*Fon*), "Close" (*Bi*), "Drag" (*Lai*), "Yell" (*Jiaw*), "Follow" (*Shuenn*), "Send" (*Shon*), "Adhere" (*Jan*), "Sticking" (*Nien*), "Rend" (*Ban*), and "Attaching" (*Tiea*). The five minor key words are "Hand" (*Sou*), "Eye" (*Ien*), "Body" (*Shen*), "Technique" (*Far*), and "Step" (*Bu*). The minor words respectively imply that the Long Fist stylist must develop speed and power (hands), reaction (eyes), smoothness (body), skill (technique), and stability (steps). As the student learns Long Fist in greater depth, many of the key words will become clear in meaning.

Turning to more particular points, it has been previously stated that Long Fist specializes in middle and long range fighting. Figures 49, 50, and 51 show the different ranges, short, middle, and long respectively. Long Fist stylists, then, will usually fight in the ranges depicted in figures 50 and 51 since they represent the middle and long distances. Although Long Fist has techniques for the short range, they will usually attempt, by various maneuvers, to keep themselves and their opponents in the middle and long range where they can effectively apply their specialty—kicking. Other Northern divisions such as Northern Praying Mantis and Eagle Claw will also fight in the middle and long range and emphasize kicking techniques. But in contrast, the Southern divisions will usually maneuver to keep themselves and their opponents in the short and middle range, where they can effectively apply their specialty—hand techniques.

Because Southern and Northern divisions emphasize different modes of fighting, their techniques will generally reflect special patterns. Thus, Long Fist as a Northern division will use the hands mainly for blocking and their legs mainly for attack. In Long Fist there is a proverb that says, "Two hands; two doors shutting"—the doors or hands shut any attack to set up the legs for kicking. Southern divisions like White Crane, however, will block with the hands and attack with the hands; thus, few kicks are generally used.

Another basic point of difference between Northern and Southern divisions which can help in understanding the free fighting methods of Long Fist is the use of the jump kick. Because Long Fist and other Northern stylists work from the longer ranges, they will many times use double jump kicks to attack. In contrast, Southern divisions, while having double jump kicks, seldom use them. In addition, Long Fist practitioners and other Northern stylists will use the jump kick to attack the high regions of the body such as the head and chest; Southern division stylists will mainly kick low when jump kicking.

While there are many differences between the Northern and Southern styles, there is one basic common element. Stylists from both systems will stand low during real fighting; this particular feature is characteristic of almost all Chinese Kung Fu styles. Even though Long Fist stylists train with some high stances, in sparring they stand low.

Although Northern and Southern divisions emphasize different techniques, the factors affecting victory in free fighting are the same for both. There are eight factors that are important: speed, power, technique, concentration, reaction, strategy, experience, and calmness. The first factor is the most important and the rest are important in descending order. This book will have, at some point, touched on the development of each aspect except for experience and calmness. Experience is something that a book or master cannot teach; it must be gained by the martial artist himself over years of training. Calmness can be gained by still meditation. Many good books exist on this subject which the martial artist can read. In reviewing the other aspects, Chapter 2 covered the methods of training speed and power; Chapters 3 and 4 covered technique through the sequences; concentration is covered in Chapter 2 in the section dealing with the development of the eyes; reaction training was explained through the fighting forms in section 1 of this chapter. The Long Fist fighting strategies will be discussed in this section.

Turning to actual combat, the first thing the Long Fist stylist will do is test the opponent. Before starting any major maneuver, three important things must be discovered. First, the specialty of the opponent must be judged. Most martial artists will specialize or are extremely proficient in fifteen to twenty techniques. These techniques must be found out to effectively counter them. The appropriate counterattacks will come from the martial artist's experience and his mastery of sequences. The martial artist should view each sequence as a book which contains valuable formulas. When a certain problem arises he searches his library of books (sequences) and finds the best formula and alters it to fit his specific needs. Second, the opponent's defensive capabilities must be measured. An opponent's sense of defense will greatly influence the type of techniques which can be used against him. Third, the opponent's speed and power must be determined to avoid being trapped and overcome.

An important aspect which must be mentioned is the area a martial artist should watch on his opponent during sparring. First of all, the martial artist should avoid focusing his eyes on his opponent's hands or legs. By watching those areas, the martial artist can be easily fooled and trapped. Many martial artists will thus watch the chest area; focusing on the chest allows a good overall field of vision. Some martial artists will look

49

50

51

their opponent in the eyes, but this should be done only if the martial artist cannot be intimidated by ugly or mean looks. (A few martial artists have been known to smile at their opponents to catch them off guard.) These people can freeze their opponents by making expressions that are frightening and overwhelming because they show an extreme killing mood.

In testing out an opponent, many methods can be used, such as fakes and trial attacks. But in finding out the capabilities of an opponent, two important things must be watched. First, never use an advanced technique to test an opponent. In the beginning of a fight, an opponent is usually too wary; showing and failing to perform an advanced or special technique will give the other side vital knowledge to prepare himself against further maneuvers. The martial artist himself must not reveal his specialty too early. Second, in testing an opponent use only simple, but safe techniques. The testing technique must allow adequate defense while also not giving away vital knowledge.

Once the martial artist has tested his opponent, the next thing to determine is which door to enter through (see Chapter 2 for definition and discussion of doors). For the Long Fist stylist, the primary determination for this is the stance and forward leg of the opponent. The first general way an opponent may stand is with his right leg forward and in a false stance (any variation of Shuen Gi Bu) as seen in figure 52. For such an opponent his middle and right doors are closed because he can quickly kick in those areas. The Long Fist stylist will then usually attempt to attack through the left door. But the middle door is also sometimes attacked. To attack through the middle door, the martial artist can use Chei Twe to kick the knee (fig. 53). The martial artist must have his body back far

52

53

54

55

enough to avoid a kick from the side. If the opponent likes to kick high, the middle door may be used to attack the groin while the leg is lifted as in figure 54. Kicking to the groin is a shorter distance than kicking to the face, hence a quicker kick.

To attack through the left door, which is naturally open when an opponent stands as in figure 52, Long Fist stylists will use a special jump kick. As the opponent makes any move forward, the martial artist, who is standing with his right leg forward, jumps forward off his right leg and spins 90 degrees counterclockwise. The final position can be seen in figure 55. From figure 55, the martial artist can simultaneously kick and punch with his right leg and hand. To train for this kick, refer to fighting form 14.

A popular technique used by many opponents who stand with a false right leg is to kick straight with the back leg and then spin kick. To counteract such a maneuver, the martial artist can use the mirror technique of figure 55. As the opponent begins his spin, the martial artist jumps with the spin and kicks the back of the opponent as in figure 56. Any time any opponent does a technique that uses a spin, always move to the exposed back of the opponent.

The next basic variation which can occur is for the opponent to stand in a flat or stable position as in figure 51, with the right leg forward. Attacks through the middle and right door can be effective against such an opponent, if the lead right hand is first controlled to prevent any kicks. The opponent's lead hand may be controlled by the action shown in figures 57 and 58. The martial artist fakes an attack in order to make the opponent react with a block. Next, the martial artist quickly hooks the hand down. By hooking the hand down, the opponent cannot lift his leg for kicking.

56

57

58

59

Once the lead hand is controlled, the martial artist can kick with his right leg to the knee (fig. 59), or kick with his left leg to the knee (fig. 60), or kick to the waist with the right leg (fig. 61). With the last technique, the martial artist must be careful that the opponent does not have the chance to kick into his groin.

Various hand techniques that attack through the right door also exist. In the first technique, once the right lead hand is controlled, the martial artist steps forward with his left leg and hits the waist with the edge of his palm as in figure 62. Next, the martial artist steps through with his right leg and strikes the jaw with the palm (fig. 63), and then quickly strikes the groin with the same hand (fig. 64). In the second hand technique, the martial artist controls the opponent's lead hand and then steps forward with the left leg while the left hand takes control of the opponent's lead arm (fig. 65). Next, the martial artist quickly spins clockwise striking the opponent in the head with the right fist (fig. 66).

An important kick which is used from the long range to attack an opponent is Shian Fon Twe, the Tornado kick. To use this kick, the martial artist first steps forward with the left leg as in figure 67. Next, the martial artist steps again with the right leg to the side (fig. 68), after which the martial artist quickly kicks Shian Fon Twe with the right leg (fig. 69). By starting the kick from the long range, the martial artist may fool the opponent into reacting too slowly to avoid the kick.

60

61

62

63

64

65

66

67

68

69

The third situation which can occur is for the opponent to stand with the left leg forward in a false stance. By standing with the right leg forward, the martial artist can effectively use some of the same techniques as in the earlier situations. The martial artist can kick the lead leg with Chei Twe as an example of an attack through the middle door (fig. 70). In addition, the martial artist may use the same kick as in figure 54 to attack the groin against high kicks (fig. 71). An extremely effective technique against an attacking left-legged opponent is to jump to the side with the right leg and to kick with the right leg (fig. 72); this is the same method as in figure 56. The martial artist himself may switch to the left leg and apply earlier techniques, but change the directions to fit the left side. Fighting form 13 in the previous section covers the practice of this kick.

The final position which can occur is for the opponent to stand with the left leg forward in a stable stance. The three techniques mentioned in the previous paragraph may be used against this type of opponent. In addition, the martial artist may switch to a left-leg-forward stance and apply all the hand techniques that were discussed against an opponent standing in a stable right-leg-forward position.

With constant practice the martial artist will find all these techniques to be effective against a wide range of opponents. To further his store of techniques, the martial artist should discuss and research with others the forms that are within the sequences. The techniques within the sequences will offer many new techniques only if the martial artist can learn to make them alive.

70

71

72

CHAPTER 6
CONCLUSION

In studying this book, the student should realize that the martial techniques presented are representative of the fundamental and middle levels of Long Fist Kung Fu in terms of barehand techniques. Much more exists to be studied. Another four barehand sequences exist which are advanced in their techniques; these four advanced sequences are extremely famous and have been practiced for, in some cases, hundreds of years. In addition, Long Fist Wu Su has a number of weapons, including narrow blade sword, wide blade sword, three sectional staff, two wide blade swords, spear, and rod. (The authors plan to write another volume on Long Fist which will focus solely on the style's weapons. The volume will include material such as the history and development of certain weapons, weapon free fighting, and weapon sequences.)

To complement the fundamental and middle level nature of this book, the authors have only presented the more popular and fundamental strategies and techniques of Long Fist free fighting. Martial artists from other styles can, for this reason, easily incorporate some techniques into their system of fighting. To incorporate the more advanced levels of Long Fist free fighting will require a study of Long Fist as a whole and mastery of the advanced sequences.

Last, because Long Fist specializes in kicking, the martial artist should study various hand techniques in order to complement the kicking. Many Southern divisions can offer valuable new hand techniques. One aspect of hand techniques which the martial artist should be familar with are the techniques of seizing and grasping known as Chin Na. Dr. Yang's book on this subject, *Shaolin Chin Na: The Seizing Art of Kung Fu,* is a systematic study of the training methods and techniques of Chinese Wu Su Chin Na techniques.

ABOUT THE AUTHORS

Dr. Yang Jwing-Ming

Dr. Yang Jwing-Ming was born in Taiwan, Republic of China, in 1946. He started his Wu Su training at the age of fifteen under the White Crane (Pai Huo division) Master Cheng Gin-Gsao. In thirteen years (1961–1974) of study under Master Cheng, Dr. Yang learned and became an expert in White Crane defense and attack techniques, Chin Na, massage, and herbal treatment. At age sixteen, Dr. Yang began the study of Tai Chi Chuan (Yang's division) under Master Kao Tao. After learning from Master Kao, Dr. Yang continued his study and research of Tai Chi Chuan with several masters in Taipei. In Taipei he became qualified for the teaching of Tai Chi. He has especially mastered the Tai Chi barehand sequence, pushing hands, the two-man fighting sequence, the narrow and wide blade Tai Chi sword, and internal power development.

When Dr. Yang was eighteen years old he entered Tamkang College at Taipei Hsien to study physics. In college, he began the study of Long Fist (*Chang Chuan*) with Master Li Mao-Ching at the Tamkang College Kuo Su Club (1964–1968). Dr. Yang eventually became an assistant instructor under Li Mao-Ching. In 1971, he completed his M.S. degree in physics at the National Taiwan University, and then served in the Chinese Air Force from 1971–1972. In the service, Dr. Yang taught physics at the Junior Academy of the Chinese Air Force while also teaching Wu Su. After being honorably discharged in 1972, he returned to Tamkang College to teach physics and resume study under Master Li Mao-Ching. Additionally, from 1968–1970, Dr. Yang taught Wu Su at Pan Chiao Senior High School, and from 1968–1971 at Chien Kuo Senior High School.

In 1974, Dr. Yang came to the United States to study mechanical engineering at Purdue University. Upon the request of a few students, Dr. Yang began to teach Kung Fu with the result that the Purdue University Chinese Kung Fu Research Club was founded in the spring of 1975. While at Purdue, Dr. Yang also taught college-credited courses of Tai Chi Chuan. In May of 1978, he was awarded a Ph.D. in mechanical engineering from Purdue. Currently, Dr. Yang has an engineering position in Houston, Texas. Dr. Yang and his co-author, Mr. Bolt, are also teaching Kung Fu together in Houston.

In summary, Dr. Yang has been involved in Chinese Kung Fu (Wu Su) for eighteen years. During this time he has spent thirteen years learning Shao Lin White Crane (Pai Huo), Shao Lin Long Fist (Chang Chuan), and Tai Chi Chuan. In terms of instructional experience, Dr. Yang has twelve years of experience: seven years in Taiwan and five years at Purdue University.

Jeffery A. Bolt

Jeffery Bolt was born in Cincinatti, Ohio, in 1956. In 1975, while studying interdisciplinary engineering (IDE) at Purdue University, he joined the Purdue University Chinese Kung Fu Research Club to study under Dr. Yang. After three years of general instruction, Dr. Yang accepted him as a "formal student," which entailed special training in various aspects of Wu Su. Mr. Bolt has especially developed the kicking techniques of Long Fist. At that time Mr. Bolt became an assistant instructor in the club to help with the teaching of Shao Lin Wu Su and Tai Chi Chuan. In December of 1978, he received his Bachelor of Science in engineering management. Currently, Mr. Bolt has an engineering position in Houston, Texas.

Master Yang Jwing-Ming

Instructor Jeffery A. Bolt

233

LIST OF CHINESE CHARACTERS

PREFACE

楊俊敏 Yang Jwing-Ming
白鶴門 Pai Huo Division
李茂清 Li Mao-Ching
曾金灶 Cheng Gin-Gsao
高濤 Kao-Tao
長拳 Chang Chuan
氣 Chi
鐵砂手 Iron Sand Hand
連步拳 Lien Bu Chuan
工力拳 Gung-Lin Chuan
一路埋伏 Yi Lu Mei Fu
十字趟 Shih Tzu Tan
趟 Tan
解 Gieh
對式 Fighting Forms

CHAPTER 1

功 Kung
夫 Fu
武術 Wu Su
孔子 Confucius
武壇 Wu Tan
少室山 Shao Shih Mountain
登封縣 Teng Fon Hsien
河南省 Huo Nan Province
魏 Wei
跋陀法師 Pao Jaco
梁朝 Liang Dynasty
達磨 Da Mo
洗髓經 Shi Sui Ching
易筋經 Yi Gin Ching
周朝 Chou Dynasty

隋 Sui
明人捕盗術 Seizing Technique of Ming People
柔術 Soft Technique
陳元贇 Chen Yuan-Yen
清朝 ChinDynasty
孫逸仙 Sun Yet-Sen
蔣介石 Chiang Kai-Shek
北伐 Northern Expedition
馮玉祥 Fong Yu Hsiang
樊鍾秀 Farn Chung-Shiow
石友三 Shih Yeou-Shan
妙興 Meaw Shing
樊軍 Farn's Army
霍元甲 Huo Yuen-Jar
天津 Tieu Tsin
精武會 Chin Woo Association
陳于正 Chen Zhih-Zeng
鷹爪門 Eagle Division
羅光玉 Lo Kuan-Yu
北螳螂拳 Northern Praying Mantis
耿霞光 Geeng Cia-Kuan
形意門 Hsing Yi Division
吳鑑泉 Wu Chien-Chuan
南京中央國術館 Nanking Central Kuo Su Institute
張之江 Chang Chih-Chiang
國術 Kuo Su
顧汝章 Gu Zou-Chang
萬顏聲 Won Lai-Shen
傅振嵩 Fu Chan-Song
王少周 Wong Shao-Chou

234

李先五 Li Shan-Wu
北少林 North Shao-Lin
自然門 Nature Division
八卦掌 Pa Gua Division
梨花槍 Li Far Spear
潭腿門 Tan Twe Division
耿德海 Geeng Dar-Hai
大聖門 Ta Shan Division
童英傑 Don Ien-Gieh
楊家太極拳 Yang's Tai Chi Chuan
孫玉峯 Shun Yu-Fon
羅漢門 Lo Han Division
李任潮 Li Zen-Chao
林陰棠 Lin In-Tan
吳家拳 Mou Cah Chuan Division
譚三 Tan Shan
蔡李佛派 Chai Li Fou Division
林耀桂 Lin Yaw-Kuai
龍形派 Dragon Style Division
張禮泉 Chang Li-Chuan
白眉派 White Brow Division
林世榮 Lin Shih-Zon
洪家拳 Hung Gar Division
吳肇鐘 Wu Gsao-Jon
師父 Si Fu
徒弟 Tuo Di
師兄 Si Shon
師弟 Si Di
韓慶堂 Han Ching-Tan
北螳螂 Northern Praying Mantis
傅家賓 Fu Jar-Bin
孫臏拳 Sun Bin Chuan
高芳先 Kao Fan-Shien
九連山 Jeou Lien Mountain
圓龍縣 Pu Zon Hisien
福建省 Fu Chien Province
黃河 Yellow River
大聖劈掛 Ta Shan Pi Kwa
查拳 Cha Chuan
羅漢 Lo Han
鷹爪 Eagle Claw
北螳螂 Northern Praying Mantis
吳家 Mou Cha
蔡李佛 Chai Li Fou

龍形 Dragon
洪家 Hung gar
白眉 White Brow
白鶴 White Crane
猴拳 Monkey
虎拳 Tiger
南螳螂 Southern Praying Mantis
詠春 Wing Chun
太極 Tai Chi
形意 Hsing Yi
八卦 Pa Kwa
六合八法 Lieu Huo Ba Far
式 Shih
招 Dsao
趟 Tan
套 Tao
對手 Twe Sou
殺氣 Sar Chi
對式 Twe Shih
對趟 Twe Tan
對手 Twe Tse
散手 Sun Sou
金鐘罩 Gin Chung Tsao
鐵布衫 Tiea Bu Shan
氣 Chi
穴 Cavities
經 Meridian
鐵砂手 Iron San Hand
硃砂手 Red Sand Hand

CHAPTER 2
馬步 Ma Bu
蹬山步 Deng San Bu
坐盤步 Dsao Pan Bu
四六步 Ssu Lieu Bu
伏虎步 Fu Hu Bu
武松 Wu Shong
金雞獨立 Gin Gi Du Li
玄機步 Sheun Gin Bu
吞步 Tun Bu
麒麟步 Chi Lin Bu
坐蹲 Dsao Dun
門 Men
空門 Kun Men
閉門 Bi Men

行步 Hsing Bu	双推掌 Shoun Tuei Chang
踩腿 Chai Twe	肘頂 Zou Den
躍步 Yiou Bu	外橫肘 Whye Hen Zou
跳步 Tiao Bu	拍掌 Pie Chang
蟬步 Shei Bu	肩頂 Gen Den
鶴跳 Hao Tiao	踢 Tie
麒麟跳 Chi Lin Tiao	蹬 Teng
縱跳 Tzon Tiao	頂 Den
單跳 Dan Tiao	脚後根 Chiao Hou Gan
拳 Chuan	勾 Kou
鎚手 Chui Sou	切 Chieh
工手 Gung Sou	掃 Shao
單指節 Dan Tzu Gieh	膝 Shi
掛拳 Kua Chuan	腿架 Tuei Jai
丹手 Dau Sou	臀頂 Tun Den
鷹嘴 Ien Jsui	踢腿 Ti Twe
鶴嘴 Huo Jsui	蹬腿 Teng Twe
螳螂手 Tan Lan Sou	切腿 Chei Twe
鷹爪 Ieu Chao	前頂 Chan Ding
鶴爪 Huo Chao	側頂 Tseh Ding
龍爪 Don Chao	膝頂 Shi Ding
豹爪 Bao Chao	外擺 Whye Bie
虎爪 Fu Chao	內擺 Nei Bie
鶴翅 Huo Chiz	掃腿 Shao Twe
掌 Chang	側踢 Tseh Tie
刺 Chiz	後蹬腿 Hou Teng Twe
手刀 Sou Dau	馬腿 Ma Twe
劍訣 Chien Chueh	跳踢腿 Tiao Ti Twe
前臂 Chien Bie	跳蹬腿 Tiao Teng Twe
肘 Zou	跳內擺 Tiao Nei Bie
肩 Geu	旋風腿 Shain Fon Twe
母子手 Mother-Son Hand	跳側切腿 Tiao Tseh Chei
平拳 Pin Chuan	蹓腿 Lieu Twe
立拳 Li Chuan	跳後蹬腿 Tiao Hou Teng Twe
搧拳 Bon Chuan	馬後蹬腿 Ma Hou Teng Twe
下搧拳 Sha Bon Chuan	八步趕蟬 Ba Bu Gan Chan
反手拳 Fan Sou Chuan	掃棠腿 Shao Tan Twe
鑽手拳 Zuan Sou Chuan	双脚蹬 Shuang Chao Teng
鎚手 Chuai Sou	踩腿 Chai Twe
双手拳 Shoun Sou Chuan	跷腿 Chao Twe
內橫肘 Nei Hen Zou	後拆腿 Hou Chai Twe
手刀 Sou Dau	百把抓 Bai Bar Chuan
橫切 Hen Chieh	磨手 Mou Sou
上翻手 Shan Fan Sou	童子拜佛 The Child Worshipping the Buddha
推掌 Tuei Chang	

百會 Baihui
督脈 Du Mei
太陽 Taiyang
胃經 Wei Ching
耳門 Erhmen
三焦經 Sanjiao Ching
眼 Ien
鼻梁 Biliang
任脈 Jen Mei
頰車 Jiache
牙腮 Yasha
人中 Zenzhong
天窗 Tianchuang
頸側 Gencheh
小腸經 Shao Chang Ching
廉泉 Lianquan
咽喉 Ienhou
巨骨 Jugu
大腸經 Ta Chang Ching
臂臑 Binao
極泉 Jiquan
心經 Shin Ching
膺窗 Yingchuang
將台 Giantai
乳中 Ruzhong
乳根 Rugen
心坎 Hsinkan
期門 Qimen
肝經 Kan Ching
中脘 Zhongwan
玄機 Xuanji
章門 Zhangmen
曲澤 Quze
心包經 Hsin Pao Ching
曲池 Quchi
內關 Neiguan
脘脈 Wanmei
合谷 Hegu
虎口 Fukuo
氣海 Qihai
丹田 Dantian
冲門 Chongmen
下陰 Shayin
箕門 Jimen

脾經 Bi Ching
白海 Baihai
伏兔 Futu
血海 Xuehai
條口 Tiaokou
中都 Zhongdu
解溪 Jiexi
太冲 Taichong
湧泉 Yongquan
醫風 Yifeng
天容 Tianzon
腎經 Shen Ching
啞門 Yamen
天柱 Tianzhu
膀胱經 Pan Kuang Ching
肩井 Jianjing
膽經 Dan Ching
臑俞 Naoshu
天宗 Tianzong
風門 Fongmen
鳳眼 Fonyen
膏肓 Gaohuang
督俞 Dushu
入洞 Zudon
靈台 Lingtai
背心 Baihsin
膈關 Geguan
鳳尾 Fonwye
精從 Gienchu
腎俞 Shenshu
少海 Shaohai
京門 Jingmen
笑腰 Hsiaoyao
長強 Changqian
尾閭 Wyelu
委中 Weizhong
承山 Chengshan
築賓 Ghubin
崑崙 Kunlun
公孫 Gongsun

CHAPTER 3
連步拳 Lien Bu Chuan
工力拳 Gung Li Chuan
一路埋伏 Yi Lu Mei Fu

237